Managing Editor
Mara Ellen Guckian

Editor in Chief
Karen J. Goldfluss, M.S. Ed.

Creative Director
Sarah M. Fournier

Illustrator
Kelly McMahon

Cover Artist
Diem Pascarella

Art Coordinator
Renée Mc Elwee

Imaging
James Edward Grace

Publisher
Mary D. Smith, M.S. Ed.

Author
Mara Ellen Guckian

Teacher Created Resources
12621 Western Avenue
Garden Grove, CA 92841
www.teachercreated.com
ISBN: 978-1-4206-8001-0

© 2016 Teacher Created Resources
Made in U.S.A.

Table of Contents

Introduction

Welcome to a workbook filled with fun for the very young! Each page in this book is designed to guide parents and their children in exploring and developing important skills and concepts.

The subject areas include the concepts listed and are arranged as follows:

- **Colors**—identifying red, orange, yellow, green, blue, purple, pink, brown, black, and gray

- **Line Practice**—recognizing and printing straight, diagonal, and curved lines

- **Printing the Alphabet**—recognizing letters and letter sounds; printing uppercase alphabet letters

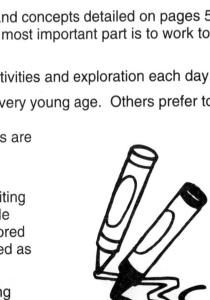

- **Math Shapes**—recognizing and tracing circles, squares, triangles, rectangles, and ovals

- **Math Numbers**—identifying numbers 1–5 and developing number sense for those numbers

- **Math Concepts**—recognizing pairs, determining more than, less than, and equal to; noticing patterns

- **Math Sizes**—comparing sizes including smaller, taller, larger, longer, and shorter

- **Thinking Skills**—learning to look at things in different ways—to compare, to sort, and to group; making choices

- **Science**—classifying animals; identifying living things; developing an awareness of body parts and the five senses; building an awareness of healthy foods; observing weather and what to wear in different conditions

- **Social Studies**—focusing on family, homes, community helpers, and work vehicles

Work side-by-side with your child to explore the new skills and concepts detailed on pages 5 and 6. Each child will develop these skills at a different pace. The most important part is to work together and to keep the following ideas in mind:

- It is helpful to balance the "book time" with physical activities and exploration each day.

- Some children are very eager to "color" or "write" at a very young age. Others prefer to observe and examine the world around them by doing different types of hands-on activities. Both approaches are age-appropriate.

- At this stage of development, most children require assistance with small motor skill activities involving writing and coloring. Don't expect your child to color the whole picture, or to stay within the lines! A few drawn or colored lines on a page are fine to start. Pages can be revisited as interest grows.

- Each page in this book offers suggestions for extending the page activity through discussion, observation, and exploration.

How to Use this Book

The *Directions* at the top of each page serve as a guide to help you and your child explore the page together. Read the directions to your child before you do each page. Here are a few tips for every activity:

- Practice listening skills and take turns discussing the pictures and the tasks.

- When speaking, use complete sentences. Work on using descriptive language. Instead of saying "I see a truck," say, "I see a huge, red fire engine." This will help your child build his or her vocabulary.

- Remember to start at the top of each page and read from left-to-right. Point to the words as you read to help your child make the connection to reading.

- Use the gray tracing lines provided to help your child practice drawing lines and later printing letters and numbers. If this proves frustrating at first, skip the pages and move on to other activities that will help strengthen your child's hand and finger muscles.

- Help your child find items, color, and count groups until he or she is comfortable doing so him or herself.

Remember—looking, listening, and thinking critically all take practice!

The *Look Around* idea at the bottom of each page was designed to reinforce the lesson by asking questions to make children think about what they are learning. Some suggestions can be done inside or while in a car, and others are best suited to outside activities—perhaps while walking or exploring at a park or playground.

For instance, if you are working on the color red, you might focus on wearing red, or you might go on a walk and see how many red cars or STOP signs you can find. Try looking for the color red in the produce section of the grocery store, too! This way, your topic will be reinforced in your child's everyday life and expand his or her view of the world.

The *Try This* ideas are provided to further enhance an activity by using added information. Many of the suggestions in this section are more physical. These types of activities offer additional support for children who need more practice to develop fine and gross motor skills.

Most of all, have fun with your child! Neither you nor your child should feel stressed if an activity seems too difficult at the time. Remember that children learn in different ways and at different times. It's okay to help your child trace, color, or identify an object with a little coaxing. The time you spend together with these activities is precious, and you will be surprised at how much your child has actually learned by the time you complete these activities.

4

Developmental Skills and Concepts

The activities in this book will expose young children to concepts and skills needed for school. Keep in mind that two- to three-year-old children are growing and learning quickly. It takes time and practice to develop the physical capabilities to sit and listen, just as it takes time and practice to learn to walk, talk, and write.

A Note about Learning to Write

Learning to write requires a certain level of muscle development, and patience. As often as possible, provide opportunities to strengthen hand and finger muscles to help young learners develop the fine-motor skills needed to use writing implements. Continually offer opportunities to work with clay, dough, small clamp-together block sets (like Lego® Duplo®), and other activities in which hands work to manipulate items.

Activities are provided to begin developing competence in a variety of areas including the following:

Color Identification

- observing and identifying colors
- classifying objects by color

Line Practice

- holding a pencil comfortably
- drawing straight, diagonal, and curved lines
- writing from left to right
- writing from top to bottom

Alphabet (prereading)

- recognizing and naming some uppercase letters
- writing some of the uppercase letters
- understanding that letters make sounds
- matching beginning sounds to objects
- observing print in writing
- repeating words and sounds; rhymes

Math (numbers and numeracy)

- identifying numbers 1–5
- making one-to-one correspondences 1–5
- identifying shapes—circle, triangle, square, rectangle, oval
- recognizing sizes—large, small, short, tall
- comparing sizes—smaller, taller, larger, longer, shorter
- making comparisons among objects to determine
  -more than   -less than   -equal to/same

Developmental Skills and Concepts *(cont.)*

Thinking Skills/Speaking and Listening

- listening attentively to directions
- sorting items by one attribute
- comparing and contrasting items
- speaking in 2–3 word sentences
- using color words to describe items
- using positional words (*in, on, under*) to describe relationships among objects

Science and Nature

- classifying animals and their habitats
- observing plants and other living things
- naming major body parts and their functions
- using the senses to explore and observe materials
- making comparisons among objects—identifying similarities and differences
- differentiating between types of weather and appropriate clothing and activities

Social Studies

- understanding the idea of family
- discussing homes
- observing community helpers and other workers
- observing different vehicles and their uses

Red

Directions: Look at the picture of the ladybug. Ladybugs are insects that help take care of our gardens. They eat bugs that harm our vegetables. Color this ladybug **red**.

Look Around: Let's walk around and find four things that are red. Name the red things we found.

Try This: Read one of the books in the *Ladybug Girl* series by David Soman and Jacky Davis. Go on a ladybug hunt in your garden this spring or make a paper ladybug and take turns hiding it in the garden.

Orange

Directions: Look at the picture of the goldfish. Goldfish are fun to watch as they swim and blow bubbles. They have fins. Color the goldfish **orange**.

Look Around: Let's walk around and find two things that are orange. Name the orange things we found.

Try This: See how many orange fruits or vegetables you can find in the produce section. Name each one as you find it.

Yellow

Directions: Look at the picture of the baby duck. It is called a duckling. It has very soft feathers. Color this duckling **yellow**.

Look Around: Let's walk around and find three things that are yellow. Name the yellow things we found.

Try This: Read *Make Way for Ducklings* by Robert McCloskey and then waddle like ducks!

Green

Directions: Look at the picture of the grasshopper. Grasshoppers have big, strong back legs. They can hop quite a long way. Color this grasshopper **green**.

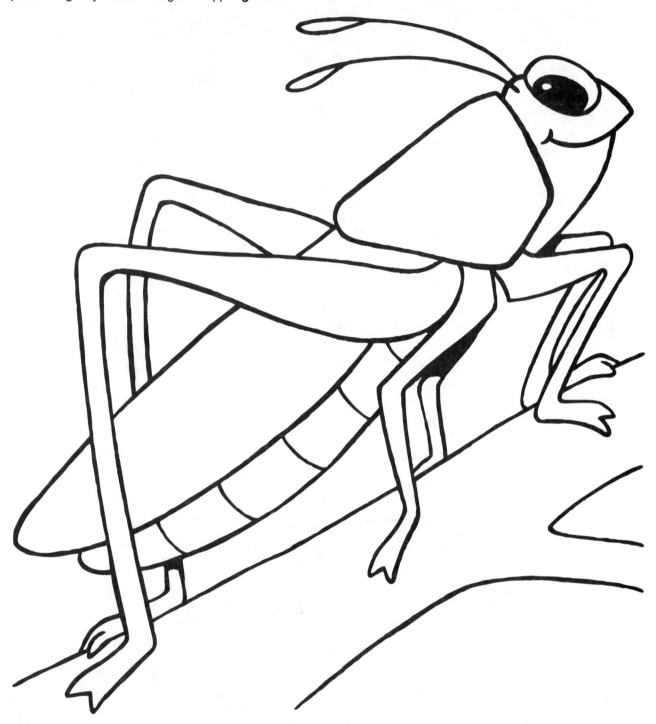

Look Around: Let's walk around and find four things that are green. Name the green things we found.

Try This: Squat down and try to take big, leaping hops like a grasshopper. Read a book about grasshoppers and learn more about them.

Blue

Directions: Look at the picture of the bluebird. Bluebirds help gardeners take care of their gardens by eating insects. Color this bluebird **blue**.

Look Around: Let's walk around and find five things that are blue. Name the blue things we found.

Try This: Find a nice place to watch birds. Watch what they do on the ground, how they eat, and how they fly. Act like the birds you observed.

Purple

Directions: Look at the picture of the butterfly. Have you ever seen butterflies fluttering around flowers? They are getting food (nectar) from flowers. Color this butterfly **purple**.

Look Around: Let's walk around and find two things that are purple. Name the purple things we found.

Try This: Pretend you are a butterfly, flap your wings and flutter around the yard. Stop and land near flowers and then flutter around some more.

Pink

Directions: Look at the picture of the flamingo. A flamingo is a pink bird with very long legs and a long neck. Flamingos are wading birds. Color this flamingo **pink**.

Look Around: Let's walk around and find four things that are pink. Name the pink things we found.

Try This: See if you can both stand on one leg like a flamingo. Can you stand like a flamingo by using your other leg? Which leg is it easier to stand on?

Brown

Directions: Look at the llama in the picture. Llamas have curved ears and long necks. They are strong animals and can help carry packs for people. Color this llama **brown**.

Look Around: Let us walk around and find three things that are brown. Name the brown things that we found.

Try This: Read one of the *Llama, Llama* books by Anna Dewdney or a nonfiction book about real llamas. Talk about the difference between storybook llamas and real llamas.

Black

Directions: Look at the picture of the sheep. Sheep can be white, red, brown, or black. Most graze in pastures and eat grass and plants. Color this sheep **black**.

Look Around: Let's walk around and find some things that are black. Name the black things we found.

Try This: Say the rhyme "Baa Baa Black Sheep" together a few times. Sing "Mary Had a Little Lamb" together. Visit a farm and observe sheep or find pictures of different kinds of sheep.

Gray

Directions: Look at the picture of the squirrel. Squirrels can be gray, red, brown, or black and they live in trees or burrows. They eat nuts, seeds, and pinecones. Color this squirrel **gray**.

Look Around: Let's walk around and find three things that are gray. Name the gray things we found.

Try This: Look at a nonfiction book about squirrels. Then, see if you can find a squirrel to watch from a distance. Notice how he goes up and down trees and how he eats.

Coloring and Printing

Coloring and printing are two very important academic skills your child will need to learn when entering school and, like most skills, they require practice. These two skills also require a certain level of fine motor skill development. To develop the muscles in his or her wrist, hand, and fingers, it is helpful to provide ample opportunities for children to use their hands.

There are many enjoyable, play-related ways to accomplish this, such as working with clay, building with blocks that connect and then taking the creations apart, and buttoning and zipping clothing when dressing. Whenever possible, allow your child to help you pick things up and put them away, fold simple pieces of laundry, and use utensils to "eat by themselves." It may take longer, but the sense of accomplishment will be worth it to your child and will help with his or her muscle development. As an added bonus, these activities are fun for a young child!

This book may just be your child's first "workbook," and it is filled with many different topics to pique his or her interests! Use the time you spend reading and working on the different pages to connect with your child in a meaningful way and have fun together exploring his or her world.

Keep in mind, that for many two- to three-year-olds, this may be their first experience holding a crayon, writing, or drawing. Be patient, as learning to hold a writing implement, such as a crayon or pencil, takes time. Use thicker crayons and short pencils, such as golf pencils, to start. Color suggestions are often made in the book to help with color recognition, but feel free to let your child choose the colors he or she wishes to use. Allow your child to use either hand and to hold the writing implement in any way that is comfortable. The goal is to get lines and colors on the page!

At first, your child may just scribble a few lines on each page. That is fine. With time, his or her strokes will become more definite and more accurate. You may wish to help color and draw alongside your child as you talk about the topics such as animals, shapes and sizes, letters and letter sounds, and numbers and amounts. Pages can be revisited as your child sees and learns more about the world. All the while, he or she will be acquiring more vocabulary and improving his or her fine motor skills.

Enjoy your time together and remember—the goal is to excite your child about learning. Take your time. Some days, your child may just want to talk about the pictures or concepts presented, and that is fine. The "writing" will come.

Trace Vertical Lines

Directions: Look at the straight gray lines on this page. They are vertical lines. Can you trace the lines with your finger? Let's try. Start at the top and go to the bottom. Then, we can trace them with a crayon.

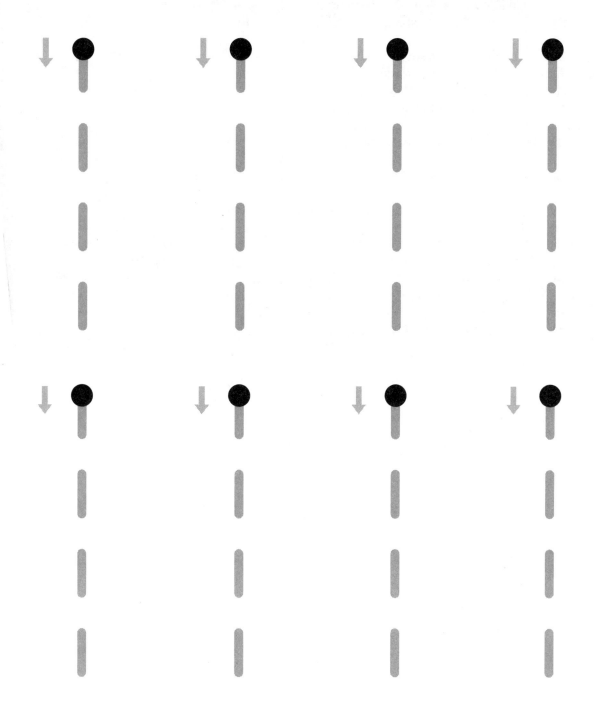

Look Around: Let us find some straight vertical lines in the house. (*edges of doors, windows*) Outside there are more straight lines to find. (*sidewalks, poles, windows*)

Try This: Prepare a tray or cookie sheet with a layer of sand or salt and have your child draw lines in it. This activity can be done over and over again drawing lines, letters, or numbers.

Finish the Table

Directions: Look at the table. It is drawn with straight lines. Can you trace the dashed lines on the legs with your finger? Let's try. Then, we can trace them with a crayon and color the drawing to finish the table.

Look Around: Look at the table legs in your home. Can you find some with straight lines?

Try This: Try to walk with your legs straight. Don't bend your knees.

Trace Horizontal Lines

Directions: Look at the straight gray lines on this page. They are horizontal lines. Can you trace the lines with your finger? Let's try. Start on the left and move across to the right. Then, we can trace them with a crayon.

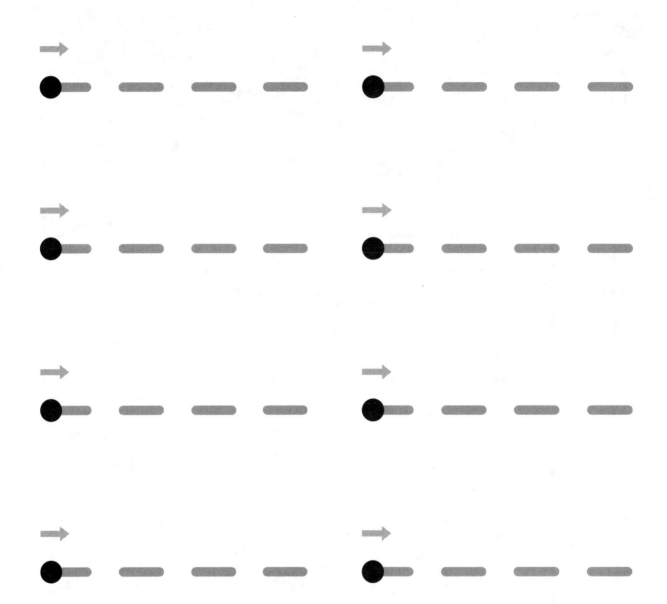

Look Around: Let us find some straight horizontal lines in the house. (*edges of tables, counters*) Outside, there are more straight lines to find. (*sidewalks, roads, roof lines*)

Try This: Hold your arms straight out to make horizontal lines.

Finish the Boxes

Directions: Look at the dashed lines on the boxes. They are straight lines. Can you trace the lines with your finger? Let's try. Then, we can trace them with a crayon and color the boxes of pet treats.

Look Around: Look at your toys. Can you find some more straight lines that go across?

Try This: Use sidewalk chalk to make big lines. Try to make them very straight.

Trace Diagonal Lines

Directions: Look at the gray lines on this page. They are diagonal lines. Can you trace the lines with your finger? Let's try. Then, we can trace them with a crayon.

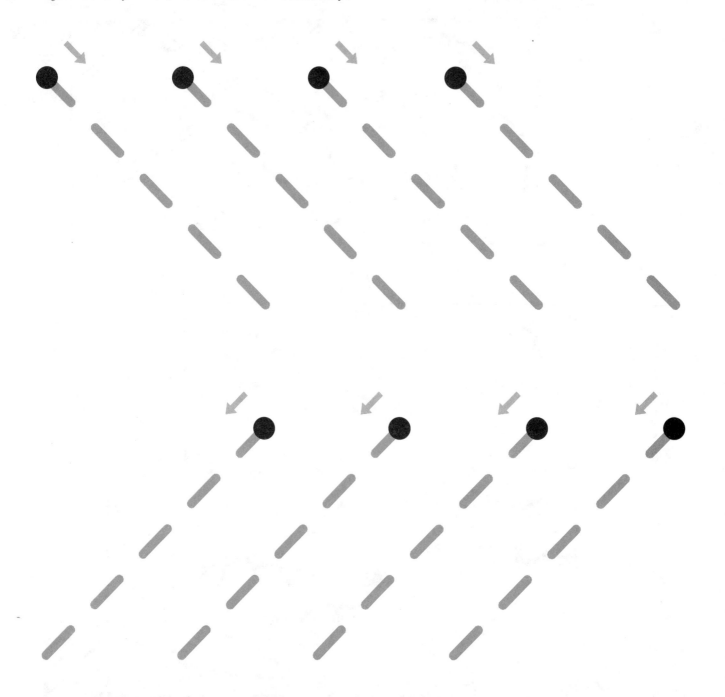

Look Around: Let us find some diagonal lines in the house. (*stair bannister, ceiling lines*) Name the objects that have diagonal lines.

Try This: Go for a walk and look for diagonal lines. While driving, see if you can spot a railroad crossing sign.

Finish the Fence

Directions: Look at the dashed lines on the fence. They are diagonal lines. Can you trace the lin[e] finger? Let's try. Then, we can trace them with a crayon. Are there any other diagonal lines?

Look Around: Let us find some diagonal lines outside. (*fences, windows*) Name the have diagonal lines.

Try This: Draw your own diagonal lines using sidewalk chalk or by using a stick in the

Curve to the Right!

ctions: Look at the dashed lines on this page. They are curved lines. They curve to the right. Can you
the lines with your finger? Let's try. Then, we can trace them with a crayon.

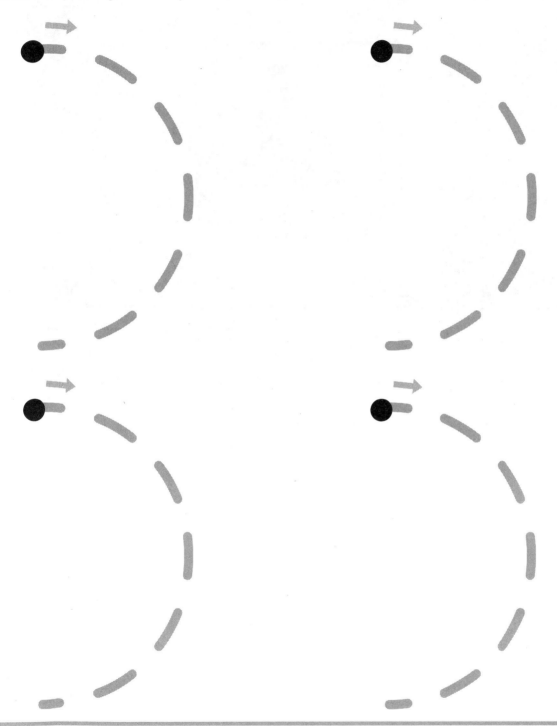

ook Around: Let us find some curved lines in the house. (*vases, glassware, lamp shades*)

ry This: Use your arm to make large curves (*to the right*) in the air. Switch arms and make more
urves. Try making smaller curves, too!

Finish the Ball

Directions: Look at the dashed line on the ball. Trace the line with your finger. Now trace it with a crayon to finish the ball.

Look Around: Wheels have curves. Wheels allow things to move. Look at different wheels. Name the item the wheels are attached to.

Try This: Sing the "Wheels on the Bus" song and do the hand motions.

Curve to the Left!

Directions: Look at the dashed lines on this page. They are curved lines. They curve to the left. Can you trace the lines with your finger? Let's try. Then, trace them with a crayon.

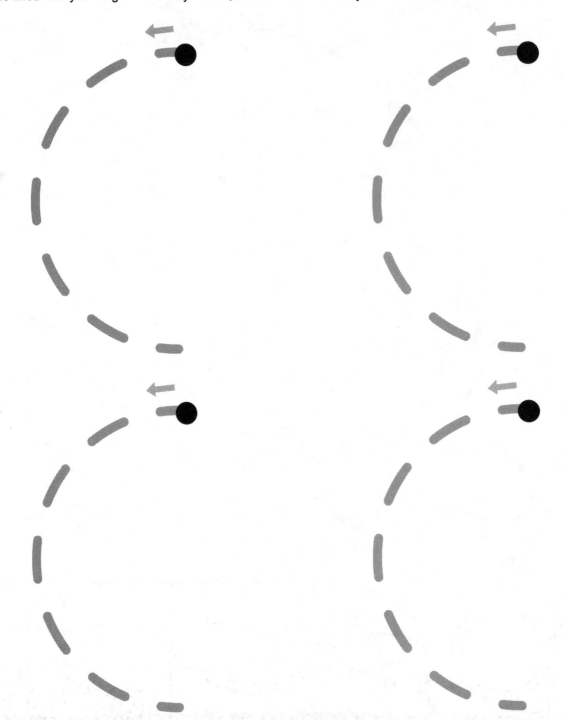

Look Around: Let us find some curved lines outside. (*windows, wheels, stop lights*)

Try This: Use your arm to make large curves (*to the left*) in the air. Switch arms and make more curves.

Finish the Balloon

Directions: Look at the dashed line on the round balloon. Trace the line with your finger. Now trace it with a crayon to finish the balloon.

Look Around: When you have dinner tonight, see how many dishes have curved lines.

Try This: Draw your own curved lines using sidewalk chalk or by using a stick in the sand or dirt.

Put the Lines Together

Directions: Look at the picture below. Can you find straight lines? Trace them. Can you find diagonal lines? Trace them. Can you find any curves? Trace them. Color the picture.

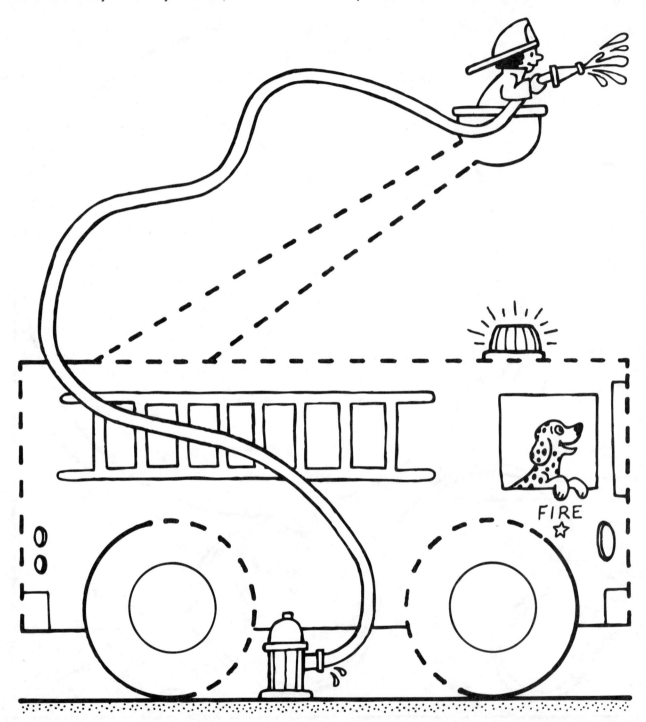

Look Around: See how many different kinds of lines you can find in your room. Name the lines.

Try This: Stand still like a straight line. Hold your arms straight up over your head. Now curve to one side and then the other. Can you make a circle with your body?

A Is for Alligator

Directions: The animal on this page is called an alligator. Alligators have large, strong jaws and many sharp teeth. They have short legs and long tails. They are good swimmers. *Alligator* begins with the letter **A**. Say *alligator* and listen to the beginning sound. The letter **A** has three straight lines. Two are diagonal and one is horizontal. Let's trace the letter **A**. Start at the dot at the top and follow the arrows. Color the alligator.

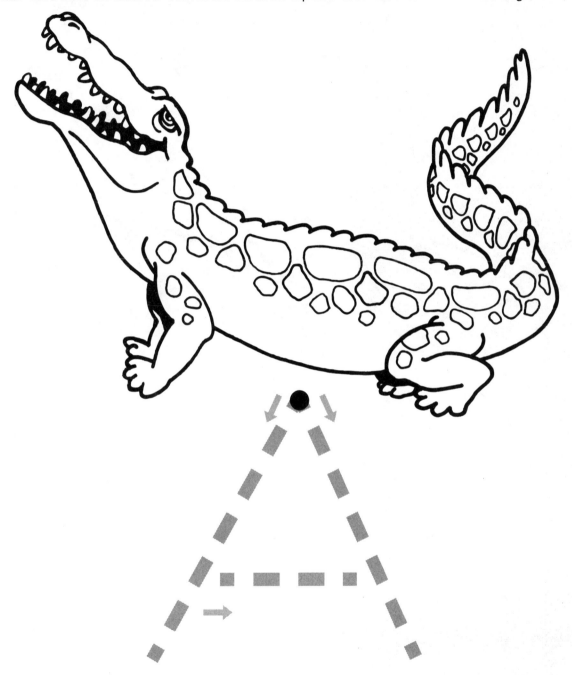

Look Around: Can you find other things that start with the sound the letter **A** makes?

Try This: Pretend you are an alligator. Stretch your arms out in front of you like the mouth of an alligator and CHOMP! Then, read a book about alligators and other animals that lay eggs.

B Is for Beaver

Directions: The animal on this page is called a beaver. Beavers swim and build dams. They are brown and have hard, flat black tails. *Beaver* begins with the letter **B**. Say *beaver* and listen to the beginning sound. The letter **B** has a straight line and two curves. Let's trace the letter **B**. Start at the dot at the top and follow the arrows. Color the beaver.

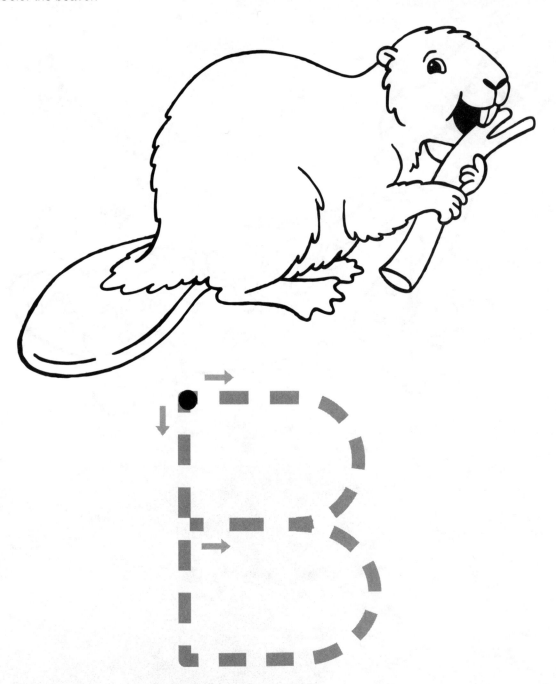

Look Around: Can you find other things that start with the sound the letter **B** makes?

Try This: *Bubble* is another word that starts with **B**. Blow bubbles and try to catch them!

C Is for Cow

Directions: The animal on this page is called a cow. Cows are large animals that live on farms. They give us milk and say, *Moooo....* Cow begins with the letter **C**. Say *cow* and listen to the beginning sound. The letter **C** is a large curved line. Let's trace the letter **C**. Start at the dot at the top and follow the arrow. Color the cow.

Look Around: Can you find other things that start with the sound the letter **C** makes?

Try This: Play or sing "The Farmer in the Dell" and see how many farm animals you can name. Visit a farm and observe the cows or take an online virtual field trip to a farm.

D Is for Deer

Directions: The animal on this page is called a deer. Deer live in the forest. Male deer are called bucks and they have antlers. *Deer* begins with the letter **D**. Say *deer* and listen to the beginning sound. The letter **D** has a straight line and a curved line. Let's trace the letter **D**. Start at the dot at the top and follow the arrows. Color the deer.

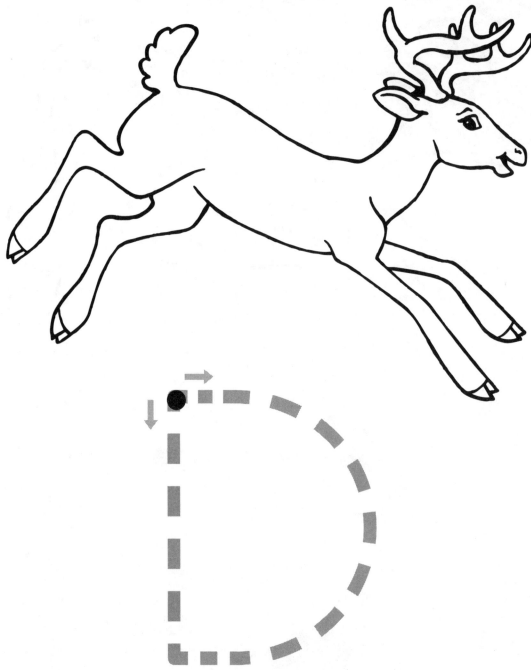

Look Around: Can you find other things that start with the sound the letter **D** makes?

Try This: *Dance* is another word that starts with **D**. Put on some music and dance around. Then, read a book about deer to learn more about them.

E Is for Elephant

Directions: The animal on this page is called an elephant. Elephants are huge, gray animals with tusks and a long trunk. They flap their ears to cool off. *Elephant* begins with the letter **E**. Say *elephant* and listen to the beginning sound. The letter **E** has four straight lines. Let's trace the letter **E**. Start at the dot at the top and follow the arrows. Color the elephant.

Look Around: Can you find other things that start with the sound the letter **E** makes?

Try This: Pretend to be an elephant. Walk on all fours and sway gently from side to side. Use your arm as a trunk and bellow like an elephant.

Directions: The animal on this page is called a fish. Fish come in many shapes, sizes, and colors. *Fish* begins with the letter **F**. Say *fish* and listen to the beginning sound. The letter **F** has three straight lines. Let's trace the letter **F**. Start at the dot at the top and follow the arrows. What color do you want to color the fish?

Look Around: Can you find other things that start with the sound the letter **F** makes?

Try This: Observe some fish in a tank, aquarium, or pet store. What do they do? How to they move? Can you move like them? Compare colors and sizes.

G Is for Goat

Directions: The animal on this page is called a goat. Some goats live on farms and graze in pastures. They give us milk. Goats are good climbers. Many goats have horns. *Goat* begins with the letter **G**. Say *goat* and listen to the beginning sound. The letter **G** is a large curved line with a small straight line at the end. Let's trace the letter **G**. Start at the dot at the top and follow the arrow. Color the goat.

Look Around: Can you find other things that start with the sound the letter **G** makes?

Try This: Read a version of *The Three Billy Goats Gruff* and then act it out.

H Is for Hedgehog

Directions: The animal on this page is called a hedgehog. Hedgehogs are small, brown, black, and white prickly animals. They have short legs and can curl themselves up in a ball to be safe. *Hedgehog* begins with the letter **H**. Say *hedgehog* and listen to the beginning sound. The letter **H** has three straight lines. Let's trace the letter **H**. Start at the dot at the top and follow the arrows. Color the hedgehog.

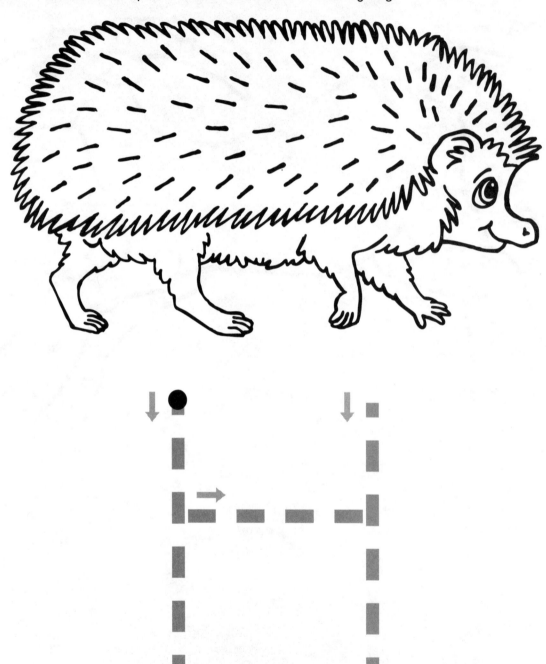

Look Around: Can you find other things that start with the sound the letter **H** makes?

Try This: Crawl around on the floor and pretend you are a hedgehog. When you hear a sound, curl up in a ball—just like a little hedgehog would. Do this a few times until you can roll up quickly.

I Is for Inchworm

Directions: The animal on this page is called an inchworm. An inchworm is a caterpillar that moves in a special way. It moves its back legs up close to its front legs and makes a loop. Then it stretches out and does it again. *Inchworm* begins with the letter **I**. Say *inchworm* and listen to the beginning sound. The letter **I** has three straight lines. Let's trace the letter **I**. Start at the dot at the top and follow the arrows. Color the inchworm green.

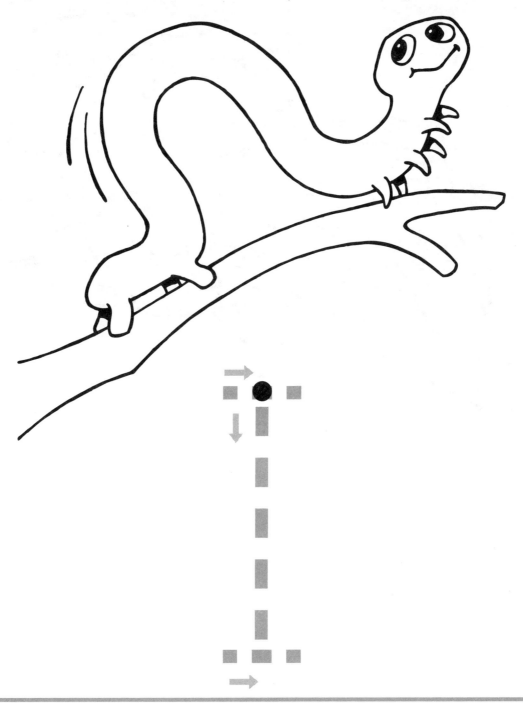

Look Around: Can you find other things that start with the sound the letter **I** makes?

Try This: Read a book about an inchworm such as *Inch by Inch* by Leo Lionni. Later, try to move like an inchworm.

J Is for Jellyfish

Directions: The animal on this page is called a jellyfish. Jellyfish float in the ocean. They can be different colors and have a top like an umbrella and long tentacles. Some are tiny, and some are quite large. *Jellyfish* begins with the letter **J**. Say *jellyfish* and listen to the beginning sound. The letter **J** has a curved line at the bottom. Let's trace the letter **J**. Start at the dot at the top and follow the arrow. What color do you want to color the jellyfish?

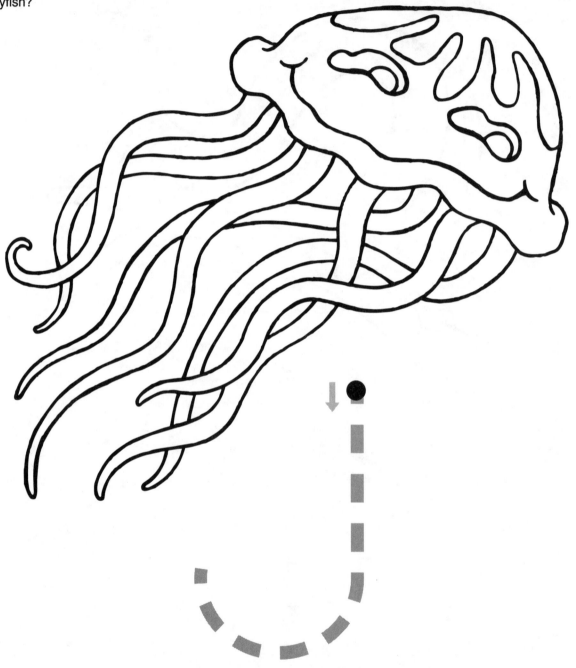

Look Around: Can you find other things that start with the sound the letter **J** makes?

Try This: *Jump* is another word that starts with **J**. Try jumping in different ways. Can you jump high? Can you jump fast and then slow? Can you jump forward and then backward?

K Is for Kangaroo

Directions: The animal on this page is called a kangaroo. Kangaroos have strong legs and tails. They are very good jumpers and can move fast. They carry their babies, called joeys, in pouches. *Kangaroo* begins with the letter **K**. Say *kangaroo* and listen to the beginning sound. The letter **K** has three straight lines. Two of these lines are diagonals. Let's trace the letter **K**. Start at the dot at the top and follow the arrows. Color the kangaroo.

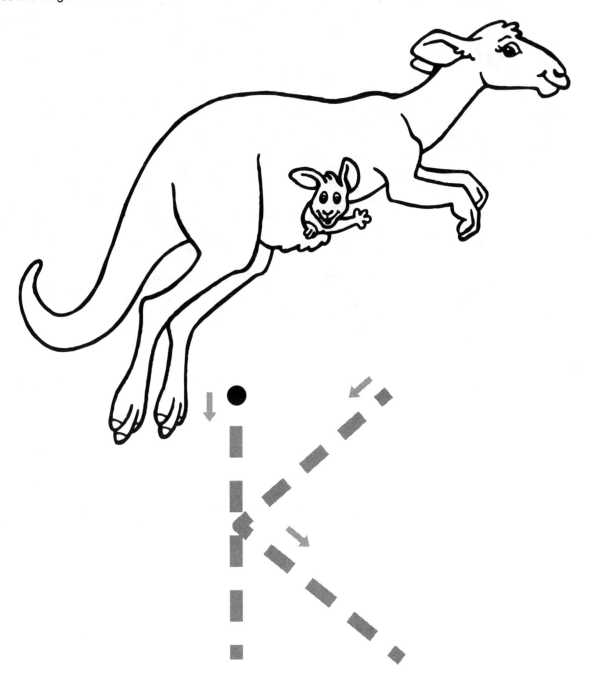

Look Around: Can you find other things that start with the sound the letter **K** makes?

Try This: *Kick* is another work that starts with a **K**. Kick a ball around and see how far it will go.

L Is for Leopard

Directions: The animal on this page is called a leopard. Leopards are wild animals. They are huge wild cats with spots, and they can move very fast. *Leopard* begins with the letter **L**. Say *leopard* and listen to the beginning sound. The letter **L** has two straight lines. Let's trace the letter **L**. Start at the dot at the top and follow the arrows. Color the leopard yellow.

Look Around: Can you find other things that start with the sound the letter **L** makes?

Try This: *Line* is another word that starts with an **L**. See how many different kinds of lines you can draw on paper or using a stick in the sand or dirt.

M Is for Moose

Directions: The animal on this page is called a moose. Moose live in the forest and have very large antlers. *Moose* begins with the letter **M**. Say *moose* and listen to the beginning sound. The letter **M** has four straight lines. Two of these lines are diagonals. Let's trace the letter **M**. Start at the dot at the top and follow the arrows. Color the moose brown.

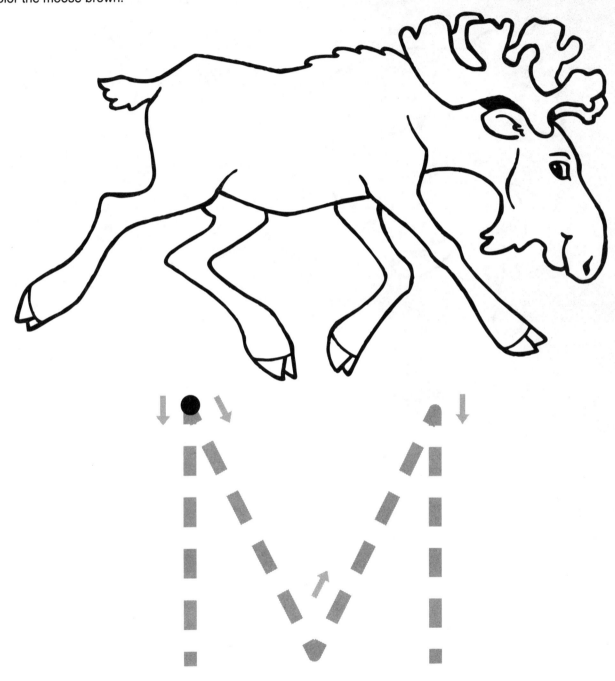

Look Around: Can you find other things that start with the sound the letter **M** makes?

Try This: Read *If You Give a Moose a Muffin* by Laura Numeroff and then make muffins!

N Is for Newt

Directions: The animal on this page is called a newt. Newts have four short legs and long tails. They live in the water and on land. *Newt* begins with the letter **N**. Say *newt* and listen to the beginning sound. The letter **N** has three straight lines. One of these lines is a diagonal line. Let's trace the letter **N**. Start at the dot at the top and follow the arrows. Color the newt red.

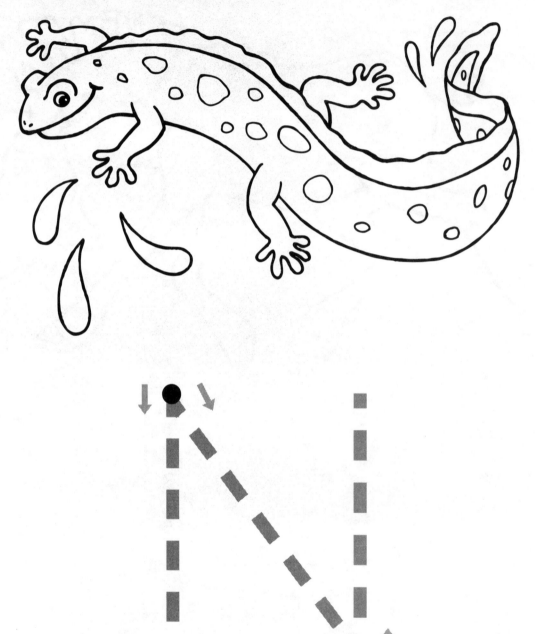

Look Around: Can you find other things that start with the sound the letter **N** makes?

Try This: *Noodles* starts with **N**. Help make noodles and enjoy them for dinner or a snack.

O Is for Octopus

Directions: The animal on this page is called an octopus. The octopus lives in the ocean and can squeeze into cracks in rocks to hide. It has two eyes and eight legs and can change colors. *Octopus* begins with the letter **O**. Say *octopus* and listen to the beginning sound. The letter **O** is a curved line that goes all the way around and makes an oval shape. Let's trace the letter **O**. Start at the dot at the top and follow the arrow. Color this octopus purple.

Look Around: Can you find other things that start with the sound the letter **O** makes?

Try This: *Ocean* and *octopus* both start with **O**. Can you find some books to read about octopuses in the ocean? Would you like to have eight legs like an octopus?

P Is for Penguin

Directions: The bird on this page is called a penguin. Penguins can swim but they can't fly. They waddle when they walk. Most live where it is very, very cold. Penguins take turns keeping their eggs warm by resting the egg on their feet. *Penguin* begins with the letter **P**. Say *penguin* and listen to the beginning sound. The letter **P** has a straight line and a curved line. Let's trace the letter **P**. Start at the dot at the top and follow the arrows. Color the wings black.

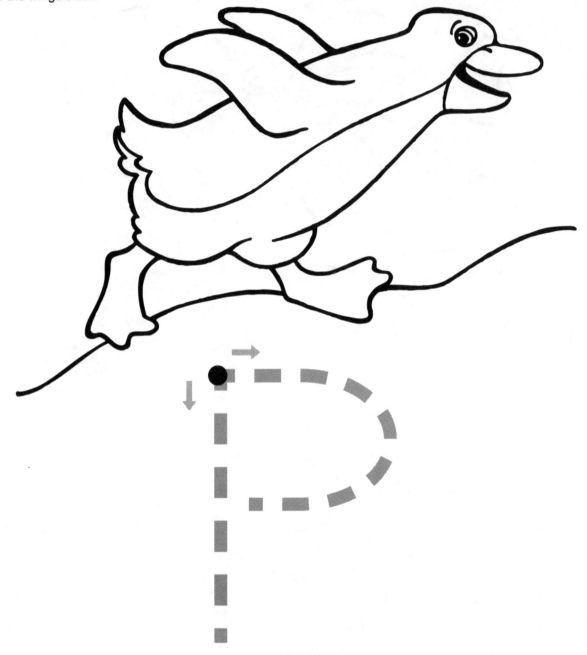

Look Around: Can you find other things that start with the sound the letter **P** makes?

Try This: Waddle like a penguin—hold your arms (*wings*) close to your sides and move from side-to-side on your feet. Pretend a plastic egg or a balled-up pair of socks is a penguin egg. Place it on the top of your feet and try to move around! It's not easy, is it?

Q Is for Quail

Directions: The bird on this page is called a quail. Quail have round bodies and small heads with a black feather on top! They spend most of their time on the ground but can fly when they need to hide. *Quail* begins with the letter **Q**. Say *quail* and listen to the beginning sound. The letter **Q** looks like the letter **O** with a small, diagonal line in the bottom. Let's trace the letter **Q**. Start at the dot at the top and follow the arrows. Color the quail's feathers gray and brown.

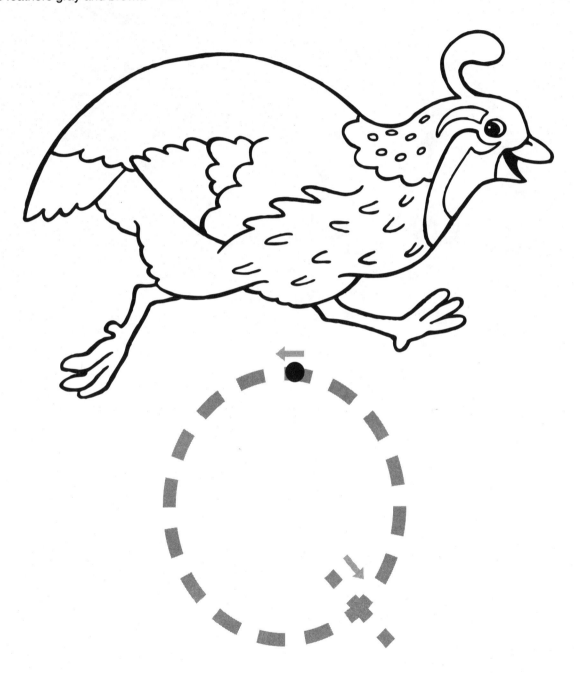

Look Around: Can you find other things that start with the sound the letter **Q** makes?

Try This: Quails move *quickly*. Can you move quickly and then slowly? Try it a few times. Scurry across the floor. Flap your "wings" quickly and then slowly.

R Is for Raccoon

Directions: The animal on this page is called a raccoon. Raccoons have gray and black fur and very bushy tails. They sleep during the day and come out at night to look for food. They will eat almost anything. *Raccoon* begins with the letter **R**. Say *raccoon* and listen to the beginning sound. The letter **R** has a straight line, a curved line, and a diagonal line. Let's trace the letter **R**. Start at the dot at the top and follow the arrows. Color the raccoon.

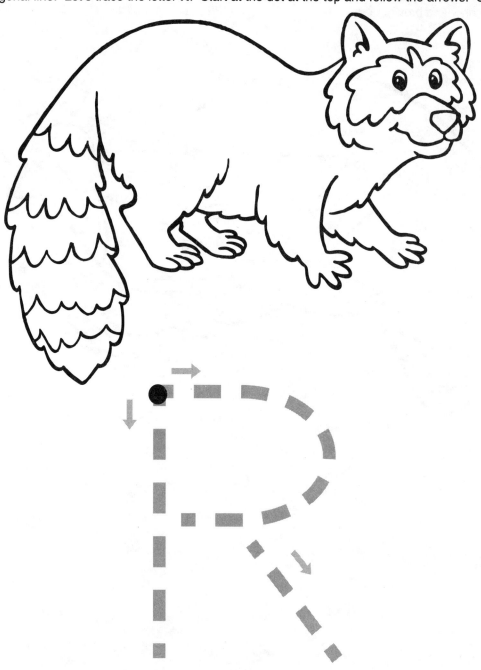

Look Around: Can you find other things that start with the sound the letter **R** makes?

Try This: *Run* is another word that starts with **R**. Have a race and see how fast you can run. Then, pretend you are a raccoon and race on your hands and knees. Which way is faster for you?

S Is for Skunk

Directions: The animal on this page is called a skunk. Skunks come out at night to look for food. They sleep in nests or old logs during the day. Skunks are black with a white stripe down their backs. They have very bushy tails. They have a bad smelling spray that they use when they are in danger. *Skunk* begins with the letter **S**. Say *skunk* and listen to the beginning sound. The letter **S** has two curves. Let's trace the letter **S**. Start at the dot at the top and follow the arrow. Color the skunk.

Look Around: Can you find other things that start with the sound the letter **S** makes?

Try This: Have you ever smelled skunk spray? Smell different food, lotions, or other items. Can you find things that have good smells? Or things that smell like a skunk?

T Is for Turtle

Directions: The animal on this page is called a turtle. Sea turtles have hard green shells and can swim in the ocean. They lay round eggs in holes that they dig in the sand. Then they go back in the water. *Turtle* begins with the letter **T**. Say *turtle* and listen to the beginning sound. The letter **T** has two straight lines. One of these lines goes down and one goes across. Let's trace the letter **T**. Start at the dot at the top and follow the arrows. Color the turtle.

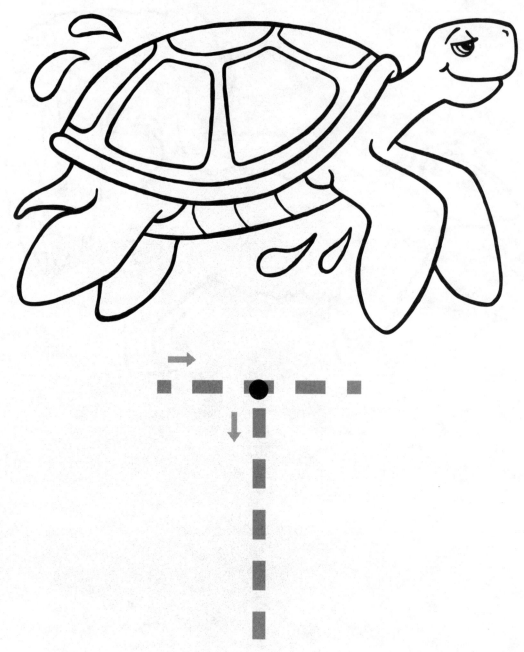

Look Around: Can you find other things that start with the sound the letter **T** makes?

Try This: *Tiptoe* starts with **T**. Can you tiptoe? Try to tiptoe for ten steps.

U Is for Umbrellabird

Directions: The bird on this page is called an umbrellabird. An umbrellabird is black with a large red spot by its neck and a crest on its head. It lives in the rainforest. It has a very loud call. *Umbrellabird* begins with the letter **U**. Say *umbrellabird* and listen to the beginning sound. The letter **U** has a curve at the bottom. Let's trace the letter **U**. Start at the dot at the top and follow the arrow. Color the umbrellabird black and red.

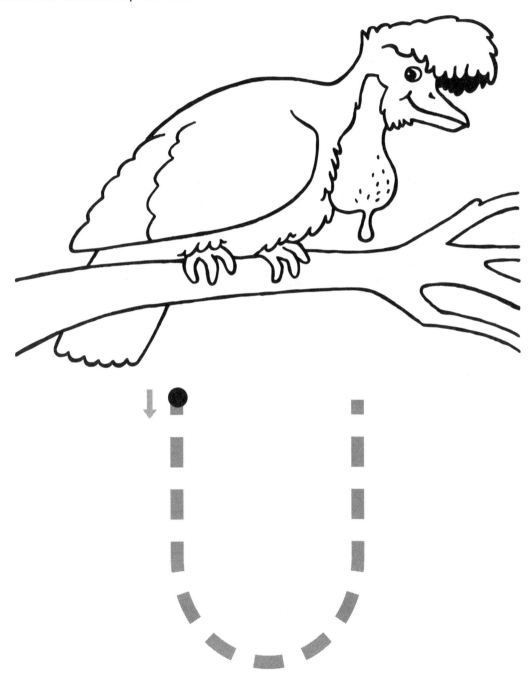

Look Around: Can you find other things that start with the sound the letter **U** makes?

Try This: *Umbrella* starts with **U**. Can you put an umbrella *up* and walk *under* it?

V Is for Vole

Directions: The animal on this page is called a vole. Voles look like brown mice but are rounder and have shorter tails and smaller ears. They burrow under the ground. Voles like to eat plants, fruits, and nuts. *Vole* begins with the letter **V**. Say *vole* and listen to the beginning sound. The letter **V** has two straight diagonal lines. Let's trace the letter **V**. Start at the dot at the top and follow the arrows. Color the vole.

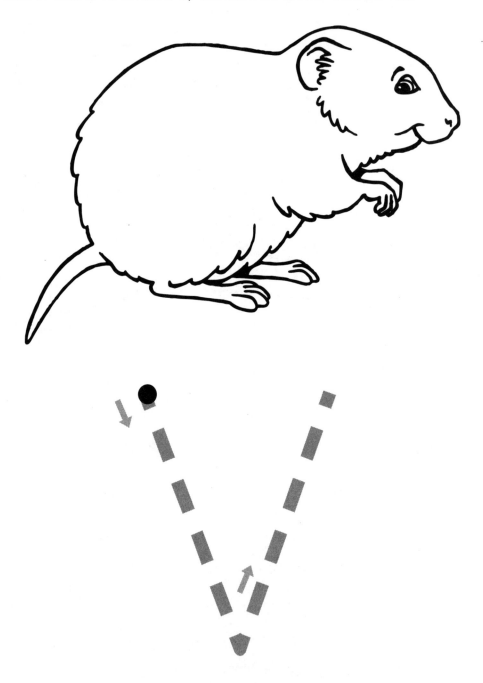

Look Around: Can you find other things that start with the sound the letter **V** makes?

Try This: *Vegetable* is another word that starts with **V**. Have a vegetable snack today. How many vegetables can you name?

W Is for Walrus

Directions: The animal on this page is called a walrus. Walruses are large animals and they have long tusks and whiskers. They use their tusks to break through the ice in the cold waters where they swim. They use their back flippers help them move on land. *Walrus* begins with the letter **W**. Say *walrus* and listen to the beginning sound. The letter **W** has four diagonal lines. Let's trace the letter **W**. Start at the dot at the top and follow the arrows. Color the walrus.

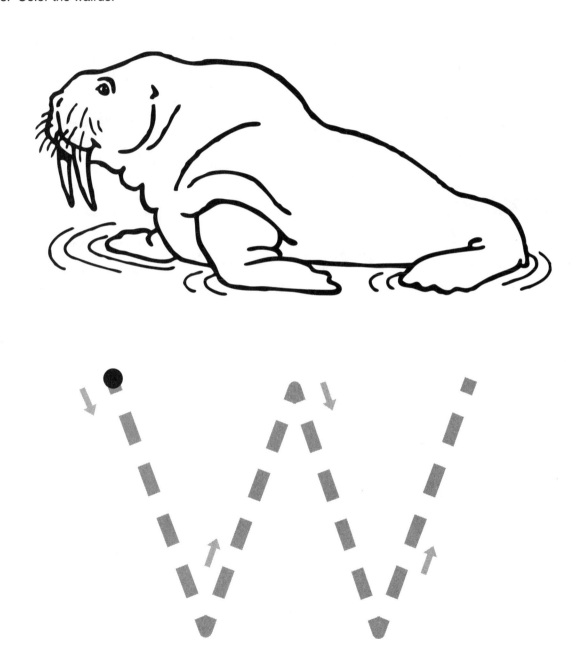

Look Around: Can you find other things that start with the sound the letter **W** makes?

Try This: Read books about walrus to learn more about them. *Wiggle* also starts with **W**. Have "wiggle time" and see how wiggly you can be.

X Is for Fox

Directions: The animal on this page is called a fox. Foxes have red, gray, black, or white fur and very bushy tails. Their ears are shaped like triangles. Sometimes they wrap their tails around them like blankets to keep warm. They live in forests and fields and sleep in dens. *Fox* ends with the letter **X**. Say *fox* and listen to the ending sound. The letter **X** has two diagonal lines that cross each other. Let's trace the letter **X**. Start at the dot at the top and follow the arrows. Color the fox red.

Look Around: Can you find other things that start or end with the sound the letter **X** makes?

Try This: *Box* is another word that ends with the letter **X**. Find a large box to play *in*. Play *in* the box and hide *under* the box. Can you crawl *around* the box?

Y Is for Yak

Directions: The animal on this page is called a yak. Yaks are black and brown long-haired animals that live in herds. They are large and have smooth horns. *Yak* begins with the letter **Y**. Say *yak* and listen to the beginning sound. The letter **Y** has straight lines. Two of these lines are diagonals. Let's trace the letter **Y**. Start at the dot at the top and follow the arrows. Color the yak.

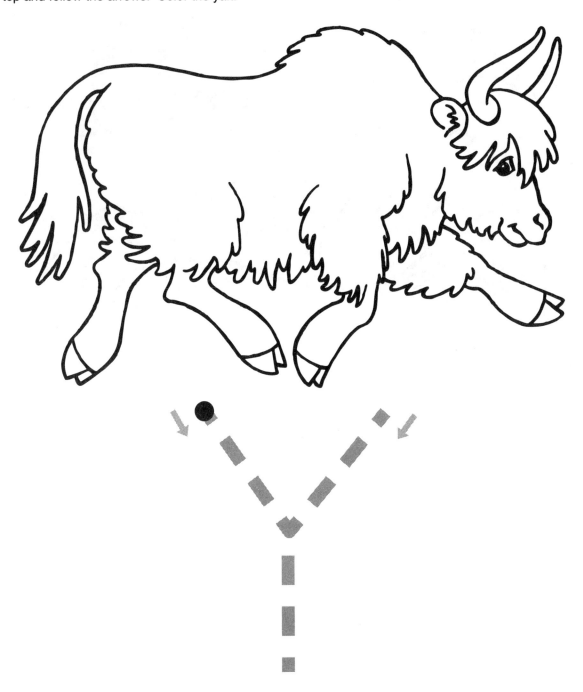

Look Around: Can you find other things that start with the sound the letter **Y** makes?

Try This: *Yogurt* starts with the letter **Y**, just like *yak*. Have a yogurt snack or yogurt for dessert.

Z Is for Zebra

Directions: The animal on this page is called a zebra. Zebras look like striped horses. They are black and white. They can run fast. *Zebra* begins with the letter **Z**. Say *zebra* and listen to the beginning sound. The letter **Z** has three straight lines. One of these lines is a diagonal. Let's trace the letter **Z**. Start at the dot at the top and follow the arrows. Color black stripes on the zebra.

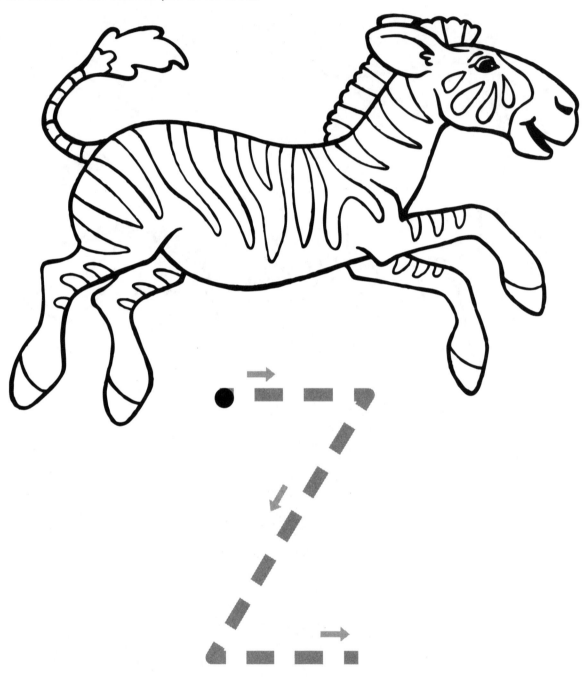

Look Around: Can you find other things that start with the sound the letter **Z** makes?

Try This: *Zipper* is another word that starts with the letter **Z**. Practice opening and closing a zipper. Zip it up and zip it down!

54   ©*Teacher Created Resources*

Alphabet Review

Directions: Look at the letters and pictures on this page. See how many your child can recognize.

Circle

Directions: Look at the shape on this page. It has no straight lines. It is a circle. The dashed line curves all the way around. Trace the circle with your finger. Start at the dot at the top of the circle and follow the arrow all the way around. Draw blue circles in the big circle.

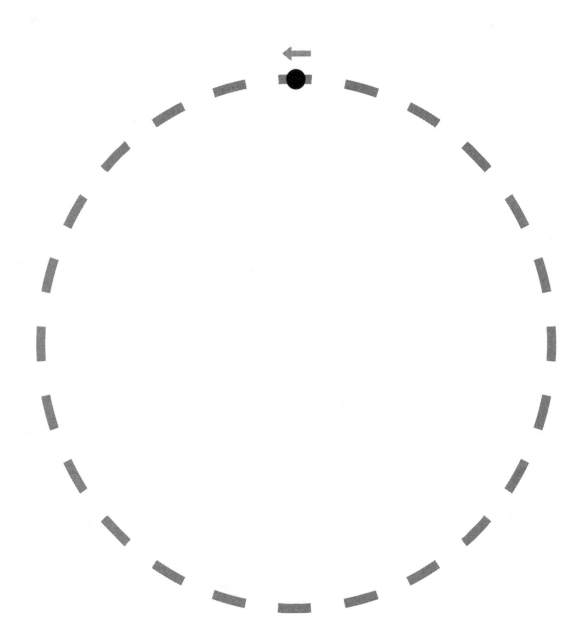

Look Around: Can you find circle shapes in the house? Are there any circles on your toys?

Try This: Make large circles in the air with your left arm and then your right arm.

Circles

Directions: Look at the different shapes on this page. Can you name them? Color all of the circles red.

Look Around: Go outside for a "Circle Walk" and see how many circle shapes you can find.

Try This: Place a hula hoop on the ground. Take turns jumping *in* and *out* of the circle.

Square

Directions: Look at the shape on this page. It has no curves. It has four straight lines and they are all the same size. Trace the square with your finger. Start at the dot at the top corner and follow the arrow. Count each line as you trace it. Draw yellow squares in the big square.

Look Around: Can you find squares in the house? Are there any squares on your toys?

Try This: Make your own squares—arrange four straws or toothpicks to form a square.

Squares

Directions: Look at the different shapes on this page. Can you name them? Color all of the squares orange.

Triangle

Directions: Look at the shape on this page. It has no curves. It has three straight lines and three corners. Trace the triangle with your finger. Start at the dot at the top and follow the arrow. Count each line as you trace it. Draw green triangles in the big triangle.

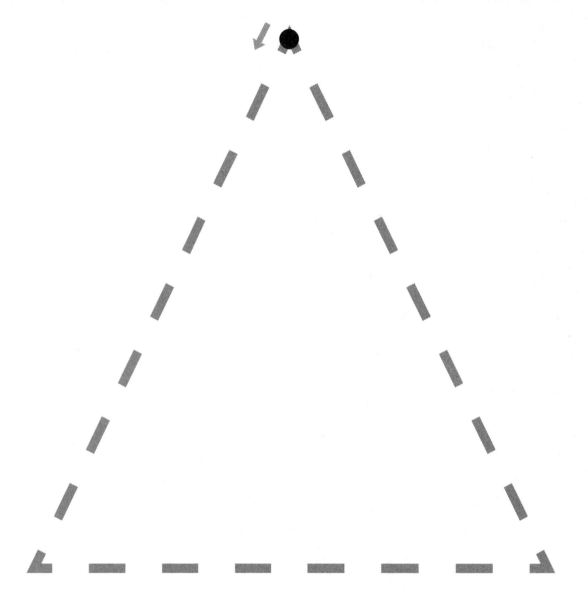

Look Around: Can you find triangles in the house? Are there any triangles on your toys?

Try This: Make your own triangles using chenille sticks, toothpicks, straws, or other straight items.

Triangles

Directions: Look at the different shapes on this page. Can you name them? Color all of the triangles purple.

Look Around: Go outside for a "Triangle Walk" and see how many triangles you can find.

Try This: Draw three dots on a piece of colored paper. Ask your child to connect the dots to make a triangle. Cut out the triangle, tape it to a stick, and make a pennant.

Rectangle

Directions: Look at the shape on this page. It has four straight lines, but it is not a square. It is a rectangle. Two of the lines are short and two are long. Trace the rectangle with your finger. Start at the dot at the top and follow the arrow. Draw orange retangles in the big rectangle.

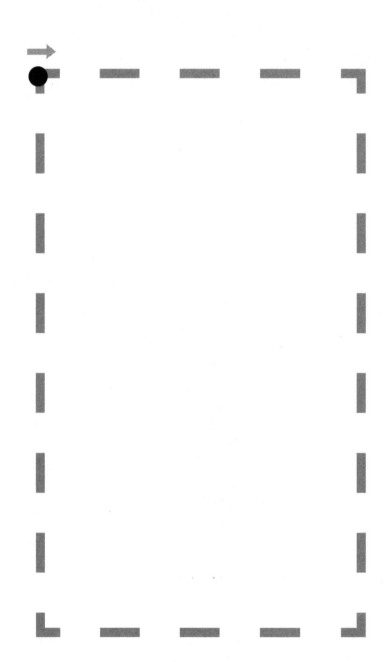

Look Around: Can you find any rectangles in the house? Are there any rectangles on your toys? Can you find some books or windows that are shaped like rectangles?

Try This: Practice drawing rectangles in the sand the next time you go to the park.

Rectangles

Directions: Look at the different shapes on this page. Some are rectangles and some are squares. Color all of the rectangles red.

Look Around: Go outside for a "Rectangle Walk" and see how many rectangles you can find.

Try This: Sort your blocks to find the rectangles. Build something with the rectangles.

Directions: Look at the shape on this page. It has no straight lines. It is an oval. The line curves all the way around but the shape is different than a circle. Trace the oval with your finger. Start at the dot at the top and follow the arrow. Draw blue ovals in the big oval.

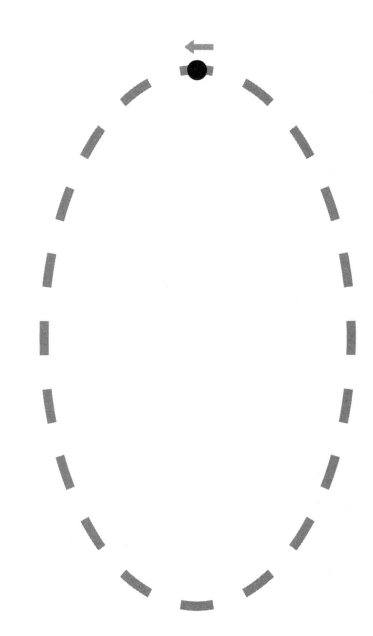

Look Around: Can you find oval shapes at home? Are there any oval shapes in the refrigerator?

Try This: Spread some shaving cream on a cookie sheet and draw ovals in it.

Ovals

Directions: Look at the shapes on this page. Some are circles and some are ovals. Color all of the ovals green.

Look Around: Go outside for an "Oval Walk" and see how many ovals you can find.

Try This: Look for ovals in the produce section. Which fruits and vegetables have oval shapes?

I Pineapple

Directions: There is one pineapple on this page. Let us count the pineapple. Trace the number **I** with your finger. Start at the dot at the top and follow the arrow. Then trace the **I** with a crayon and color the pineapple.

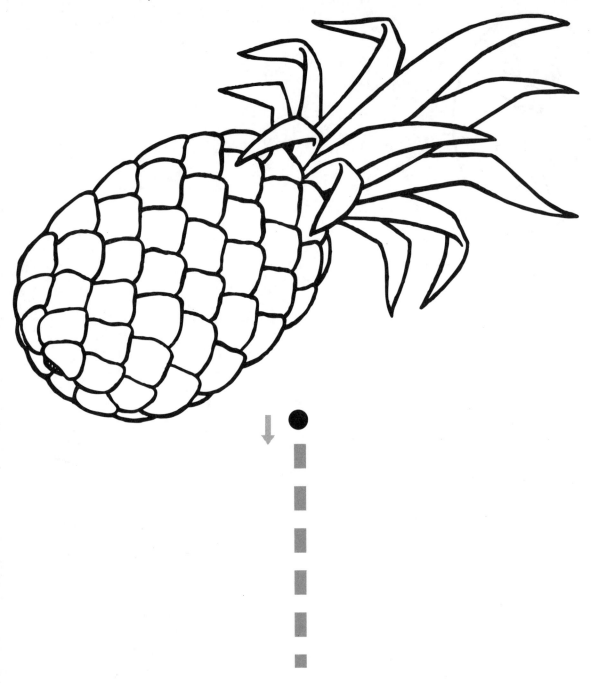

Look Around: Find one door, one chair, and one toy.

Try This: When you get dressed, see how many things you wear one of—shirt, jacket, hat, etc.

I of a Kind

Directions: Look at the toys in each row. Two are the same, and one is different. Circle or color the one that is different in each row.

Look Around: Look in the mirror. You are one of a kind! Let us see how many things you have one of—head, neck, nose, mouth, etc.

Try This: Hop on one foot and then the other foot.

2 Bananas

Directions: Look at the bananas. How many do you see? Let us count them, *one... two*. Trace the number **2** with your finger. Start at the dot at the top and follow the arrow. Then trace the **2** with a crayon and color the bananas.

Look Around: Can you find two toys? What else can you find two of in the room?

Try This: Look in the mirror. Let us see how many things you have two of—eyes, ears, hands, legs, feet, etc.

2 of Each

Directions: Look at the picture. Count the eggs. Color the two eggs in the nest.

Look Around: Can you find two blue cars? Can you find two tall trees?

Try This: Tap your shoulders two times, then clap two times, then stamp your foot two times.

3 Pears

Directions: Look at the pears. How many do you see? Let us count them, *one... two... three*. Trace the number **3** with your finger. Start at the dot and follow the arrow. Then trace the **3** with a crayon and color the pears.

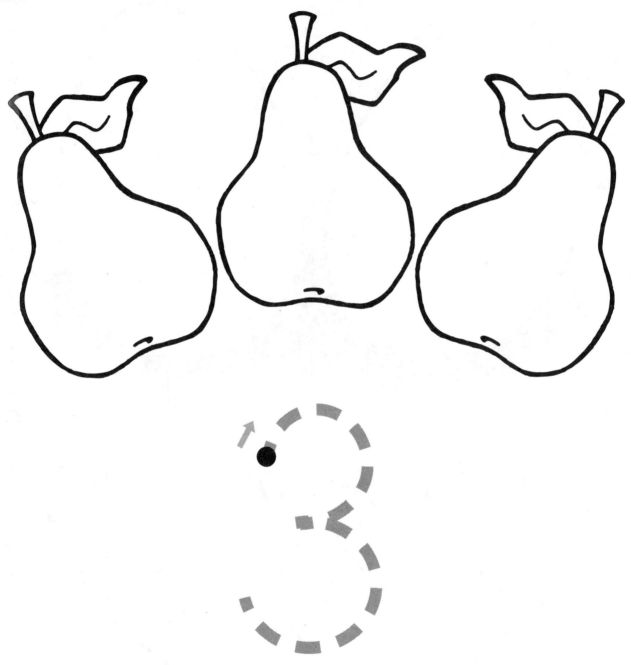

Look Around: Can you find a bike with three wheels or a stool with three legs?

Try This: Read or tell "3s" stories and rhymes such as the *The Three Little Pigs*, *The Three Billy Goats Gruff*, and *Goldilocks and The Three Bears*.

A Group of 3

Directions: Look at the picture. Count the baby birds in the nest. Color the three baby birds in the nest.

Look Around: Ask your child to pick his or her three favorite counting books and have a special reading time.

Try This: Play a clapping game. Clap three times fast and three times slow. Clap three times over your head and three times behind your back. Do it again!

4 Peaches

Directions: Look at the peaches. How many do you see? Let us count them, *one… two… three… four*. Trace the number **4** with your finger. Start at the dots at the top and follow the arrows. Then trace the **4** with a crayon and color the peaches.

Look Around: Can you find a chair with four legs and a table with four sides?

Try This: Arrange snack pieces in groups of four—four crackers, four apple slices, etc.

A Group of 4

Directions: Look at the pea pod. How many peas do you see? Color the four peas in the pod.

Look Around: Ask your child to pick up and put away four toys.

Try This: Go for a walk and see how many animals you can see that have four legs.

5 Strawberries

Directions: Look at the strawberries. How many do you see? Count them, *one… two… three… four… five.* Trace the number **5** with your finger. Start at the top and follow the arrows. First, go down and around. Then draw the straight line across. Then trace the **5** by using a crayon, and color the strawberries.

Look Around: Read or listen to "Five Little Ducks." (See page 78.)

Try This: Sing and act out the song, "Five Little Monkeys." (See page 79.)

A Group of 5

Directions: Look at the gingerbread cookies. Color the five cookies and count them. How many are gingerbread boys, and how many are gingerbread girls?

Look Around: Hold up one hand and ask your child to count your fingers. Help as needed. Then count his or her fingers.

Try This: Make handprints in the sand or use finger paint to make prints on paper. Count the fingers on each handprint.

5 Toes

Directions: Have your child place one foot at a time in the frame below. Trace each of his or her feet. Count as you trace each toe. Then, count and number the toes on the picture together.

Look Around: The next time your child has bare feet, teach him or her the song "This Little Piggy Went to Market."

Try This: Walk five steps and then walk on tiptoes for five more steps. Repeat.

1, 2, 3, 4, 5!

Directions: Look at the numbers in the column on the left. Count the stars in each group on the right. Draw a line to match each number to the correct group.

1

2

3

4

5

Look Around: Go to the produce market and see if you and your child can find 5 red foods or 5 favorite vegetables. Find stories to read with numbers in them.

Try This: Number the inside bases of five cupcake papers 1 to 5. Collect small items like pebbles or shells and help your child place the correct amount on each number in the cup.

Five Little Ducks

Five little ducks went out one day
Over the hill and far away.
Mother duck said, "Quack, quack, quack,"
But only four little ducks came back.

Four little ducks went out one day
Over the hill and far away.
Mother duck said, "Quack, quack, quack,"
But only three little ducks came back.

Three little ducks went out one day
Over the hill and far away.
Mother duck said, "Quack, quack, quack,"
But only two little ducks came back.

Two little ducks went out one day
Over the hill and far away.
Mother duck said, "Quack, quack, quack,"
But only one little duck came back.

One little duck went out one day
Over the hill and far away.
Mother duck said, "Quack, quack, quack,"
But none of the little ducks came back.

Sad mother duck went out one day
Over the hill and far away.
Sad mother duck said, "Quack, quack, quack,"
And all five ducks came marching back!

Try This: Find five toy ducks and act out the song as you sing it together.

Five Little Monkeys

Directions: Chant or sing "Five Little Monkeys" together. Encourage your child to practice counting backward using his or her five fingers.

Five little monkeys jumping on the bed,
One fell off and bumped his head,
Mama called the doctor and the doctor said,
"No more monkeys jumping on the bed!"

Four little monkeys jumping on the bed,
One fell off and bumped his head,
Mama called the doctor and the doctor said,
"No more monkeys jumping on the bed!"

Three little monkeys jumping on the bed,
One fell off and bumped his head,
Mama called the doctor and the doctor said,
"No more monkeys jumping on the bed!"

Two little monkeys jumping on the bed,
One fell off and bumped his head,
Mama called the doctor and the doctor said,
"No more monkeys jumping on the bed!"

One little monkey jumping on the bed,
One fell off and bumped his head,
Mama called the doctor and the doctor said,
"Put those monkeys right to bed!"

Look Around: Find a version of the book, "Five Little Monkeys" to read together.

Try This: Place a large pillow on the floor and have your child act out the song using stuffed animals. If you wish, change the line to "Five little *animals* jumping on the bed…".

Make Pairs

Directions: Look at the pictures. Trace lines to match the pairs of things you wear.

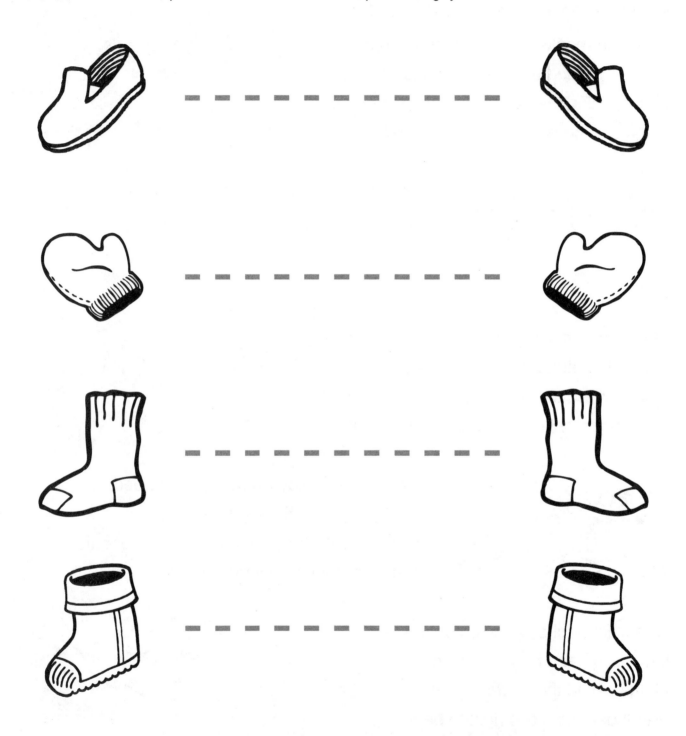

Look Around: Can you find pairs of things? (*book ends, candlesticks, salt and pepper shakers*)

Try This: Put all your shoes in a pile and then ask your child to arrange them in pairs. Ask your child to help match socks on laundry day.

More Than

Directions: Look at the turtles on the rocks. Count the turtles on each rock. Color the turtles on the rock that has more.

Look Around: Group five of your child's toys in one pile and three in another pile. Compare the two groups and decide which pile has more. Rearrange the piles a few times to keep playing.

Try This: Arrange fruit slices on two plates. Have four slices on one plate and two slices on the other. Ask your child to choose the plate of fruit that has more slices.

Which Has More?

Directions: Look at the plants in each box. Count the flowers on each plant. Color the plant that has more flowers.

Look Around: Collect five leaves and lay them out in a line. Ask, "How many leaves do you see?" Then, put two in one group and three in the other group. Ask, "Which group has more leaves?"

Try This: Arrange fruit slices or snack crackers in rows of 3, 4, and 5. Ask your child to pick the row that has the most.

82

Look at the Pattern

Directions: Look at the insects. Can you name them? Talk about the pattern you see in each row. Color the insect you think comes next in each row.

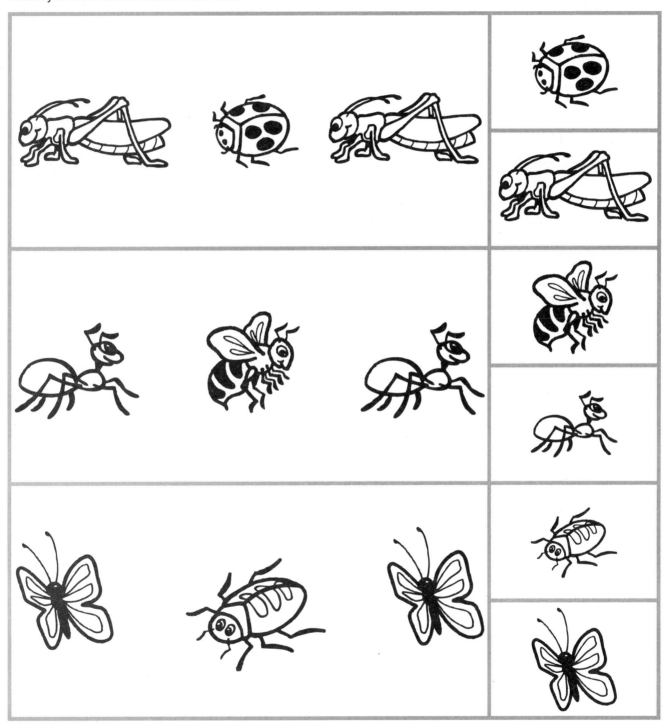

Look Around: Find an alternating pattern—perhaps stripes on a shirt or tiles on the floor. Talk about patterns.

Try This: Alternate different colored blocks or other toys and make different patterns.

What Is Next?

Directions: Look at each row and decide which shape comes next. Help your child draw that shape with a crayon.

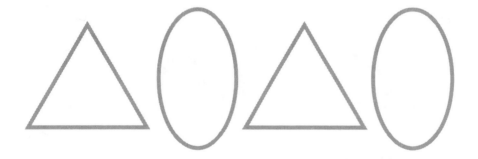

Look Around: Make a pattern. Try alternating colored objects—red block, blue block, etc.

Try This: Take different kinds of steps to make a pattern on your next walk. Take three giant steps, four baby steps, and repeat. Do this a few times to help your child understand the pattern.

#8001 1-2-3 Learn   84   ©Teacher Created Resources

Equal To

Directions: There are four groups on this page. Count each group to find the ones that have the same number of items. Draw a line to match the groups.

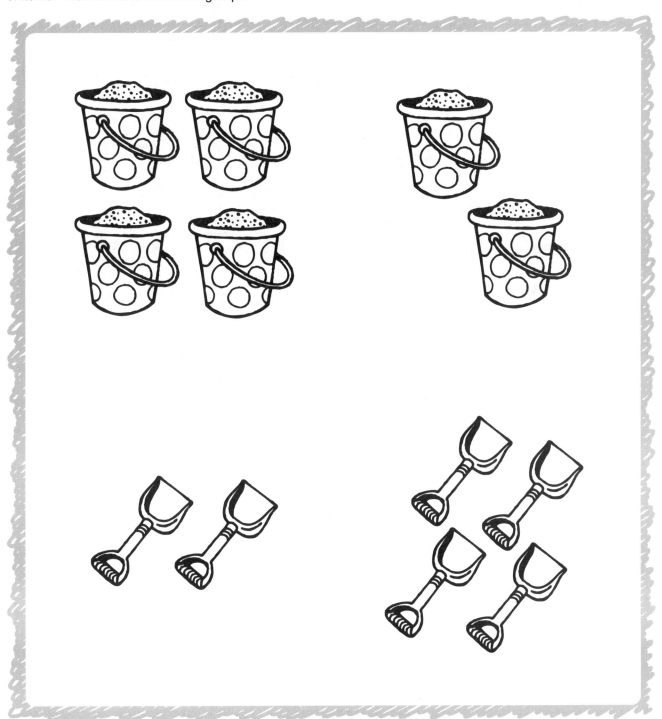

Look Around: Can you find groups of similar items to count?

Try This: Use five matching blocks, beads, or spoons. Ask your child to arrange them in different groups to review 1–5.

Equal Means the Same

Directions: Count the candles on each cupcake in the row. Color the row that has the same amount of candles on both cupcakes.

Look Around: Count the plates on the table for your next meal together. Count the forks. Ask your child to help put the same number of spoons on the table—one next to each plate.

Try This: Make small piles of fish crackers (1–5) for your child to count and match with his or her own fish crackers.

The Same Size

Directions: Look at the animals in each row. Put an **X** on the animal that is not the same size.

Look Around: Can you find things in your house that are the same size? (*dining room chairs*)

Try This: Help your child sort blocks and group them by size. Put two blocks that are the same and one that is different in a line. Have your child choose the one that is not the same size. Rearrange the order of the three items and do it again.

Which Is Smaller?

Directions: Look at the two dinosaurs in each row. Put an **X** on the dinosaur that is smaller.

Look Around: Find items to compare and ask your child to determine which one is smaller.

Try This: Ask your child to find items in the house that are smaller than he or she is.

Which Is Taller?

Directions: Look at the two birds in each box. Circle the bird in each box that is taller. Color all the birds.

Look Around: Stand next to your child in front of a mirror. Ask, "Who is taller? Who is shorter?"

Try This: Play with blocks. Make two tall towers and compare them. "Which tower is taller?"

Which Is Larger?

Directions: Look at the two boats in the water. Circle the boat that is larger. Color the boats.

Look Around: Compare pairs of things you see while walking—buildings, cars, trees, etc. Which one of each pair is taller?

Try This: Help your child compare pairs of similar items and determine which is larger. (*cars, gift bags, chairs, etc.*)

Which Is Longer?

Directions: Look at the two caterpillars in each box. Color the caterpillar that is longer in each row green.

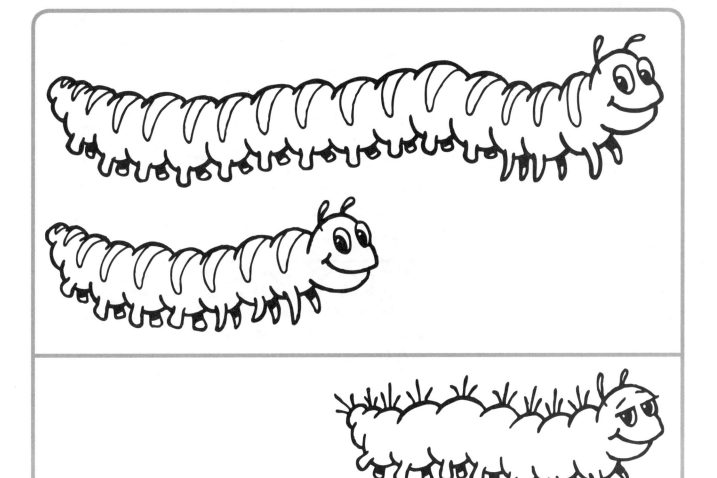

Look Around: Compare lengths of ribbon or string with your child to determine which is longer.

Try This: Cut carrot sticks into different lengths. Present two different-sized carrot sticks to your child and ask, "Which one is longer?" Do this a few times and then ask your child to pick two for you to compare.

Which Is Shorter?

Directions: Look at the locomotives on the tracks. Talk about the size of each train and compare them. Color the locomotive that is shorter black.

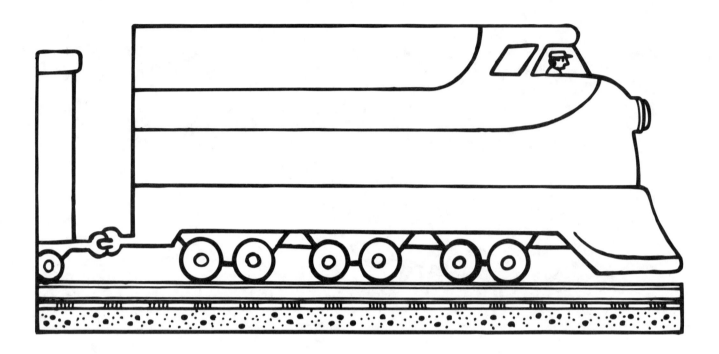

Look Around: Find two trees for your child to compare. Ask, "Which one is shorter?"

Try This: Sit down against a wall with your child at your side. Stretch your legs out in front of you. Compare leg lengths and discuss whose legs are shorter.

Big and Little

Directions: There are four sets of toys. In each set, color the toy that is **big** and circle the toy that is **little**.

Look Around: Find items in the kitchen to compare and encourage your child to use the descriptive words to describe the items—big spoon/little spoon, big plate/little plate, etc.

Try This: Alternate big and little steps when walking with your child. Discuss what you are doing as you walk. "Let's take a BIG step and a little step, BIG step, little step, …."

Biggest and Smallest

Directions: Look at the rows of cups and bowls. In each row, color the biggest item blue. Color the smallest item orange.

Look Around: Find some items in your house or yard to compare. Use words like *big*, *bigger*, *biggest*, and *small*, *smaller*, *smallest*.

Try This: Scrunch down into a little ball. Ask your child to do the same thing. Then, with your child, grow big, then bigger, then as big as you can with your arms fully outstretched and your legs as straight as possible.

Three Bears' Chairs

Directions: Look at the three bears on the left and talk about the different sizes. Which bear gets the smallest chair? Which bear needs the largest chair? Match each bear to its chair. Use a crayon to trace each line from the bear to its chair.

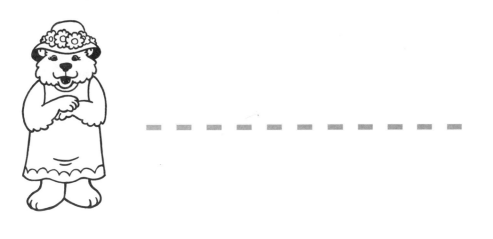

Look Around: Find two or more items, such as toy vehicles, blocks, or stuffed animals to arrange by size.

Try This: Stand family members together in front of a mirror. Ask, "Who is small, who is large, and who is in the middle (*medium*)?"

Three Bears' Beds

Directions: Look at the three bears on the top and talk about their different sizes. Which bear gets the smallest bed? Which bear needs the largest bed? Which bed is left for the last bear? Match each bear to its bed below. Use a crayon to trace each line from the bear to its bed.

Look Around: Compare the beds in your house. Which is small and which is large? Talk about the sizes. "This bed is the smallest bed in the house, and this bed is the largest bed." Are there any beds that are the same size?

Try This: Collect things that are small and things that are large. Help your child make different comparisons. For instance, collect and observe three different-sized rocks or pebbles. "This is the smallest rock, and this is the largest rock."

Same and Different

Directions: Look at each set of pictures below. Two of the pictures are the same, and one is different. Talk about what is the same and what is different. Circle the picture that is different in each row.

Look Around: Collect leaves from two trees with different-shaped leaves. Place two leaves from one tree and one leaf from the other tree in a line and ask your child to find the leaf that is different.

Try This: Line up two things that are the same and one that is different and ask your child to find the one that is different. (*three checkers—two black, one red; three blocks—two rectangles one square, etc.*)

What Goes Together?

Directions: Talk about the pictures. Trace the lines from one picture to the other. Discuss how the two items go together.

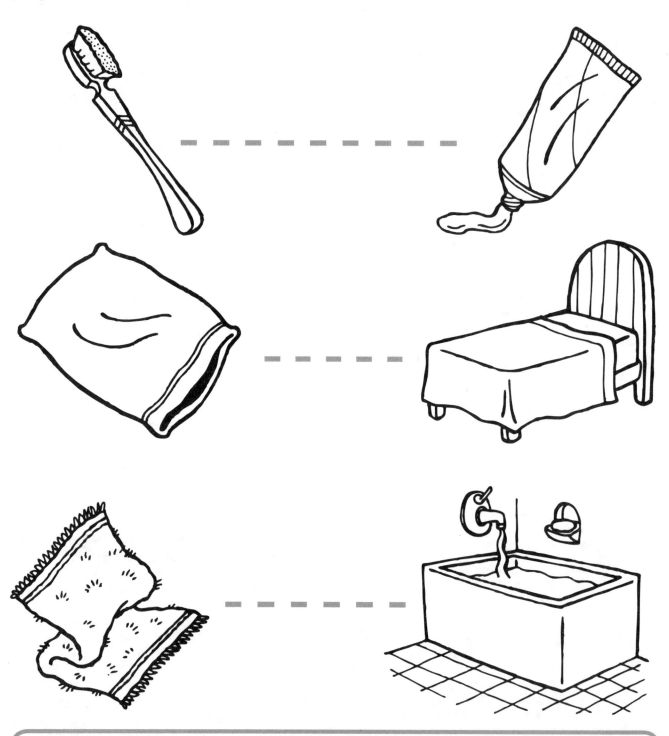

Look Around: Find things in the house that go together and discuss why they are related. (*tables and chairs, pillows and blankets, pails and shovels, etc.*)

Try This: Have a snack that "goes together" like peanut butter and jelly, macaroni and cheese, or veggies and dip.

In and Out

Directions: Look at the two frogs playing at the pond. One frog is **in** the water and one frog is **out** of the water. Point to the frog that is in the water. Color the frog that is out of the water.

Look Around: Are you in the house, or out? Together, notice times when you go in or out.

Try This: Place a ball in a basket and then take it out of the basket. Do this numerous times and practice using the words "in" and "out" each time. "The ball is in the basket, the ball is out of the basket!"

Up and Down

Directions: Look at the two frogs playing. One frog is **up** in the air and one frog is **down** on the ground. Point to the frog that is up in the air. Color the frog that is down on the ground.

Look Around: Notice things that are up like birds in the sky and things that are down like acorns that have fallen from trees. Mention when you get up and when you sit down or go up and down stairs.

Try This: Throw a ball up in the air and watch it come down. Do this numerous times and practice saying the words "up" and "down" each time. "The ball is up in the air, the ball is down on the ground!"

On and Under

Directions: Look at the two frogs playing. One frog is **on** a log and one frog is **under** the log. Point to the frog that is on the log. Color the frog that is under the log.

Look Around: What can you sit on? What can you sit under? Go on a hunt in the house find things to sit on or under. Try this activity outside. Sit on a blanket and have a picnic under a tree.

Try This: Roll a ball on a table and then roll it under the table. Do this a few times and practice using the words "on" and "under" each time. "The ball is on the table, the ball is under the table!"

On and Off

Directions: Look at the two frogs playing. One is **on** a rock and one is **off** the rock. Point to the frog that is on the rock. Color the frog that is off the rock.

Look Around: Are the leaves on the trees or are they falling off? Put your jacket on and take it off.

Try This: Play "On and Off." When the lights are on, wiggle around; when you flip the switch and turn the light off, freeze. Or hop on and off a large pillow on the ground.

Top and Bottom

Directions: Look at the two frogs playing. One is on top of the other. Point to the frog that is on **top**. Circle the frog that is on the **bottom**.

Look Around: Look at some shelves in the house. Talk about things on the top shelf and things on the bottom shelf.

Try This: Ask your child to help you put things away on the top or bottom shelf or in a top or bottom drawer.

Sort the Clothes

Directions: Look at all the clothes. Some clothes are for hot days and some clothes keep you warm when it is cold. Color the clothes you would wear in warm, summer weather.

Look Around: What is the weather like at your house? What kind of clothes will be comfortable to wear today?

Try This: Read a book about weather or seasons. Then, go back and look at the pictures and talk about what to wear in each situation.

Sort the Furniture

Directions: Look at the furniture below. Name each piece of furniture and talk about its purpose. Color the pieces of furniture you can sit on. Cross out the other pieces.

Look Around: See how many things you can find to sit on in your house. What do you sit on at the park?

Try This: Walk around the house and talk about different pieces of furniture. How many things can you sleep on? What do you eat on? Get to know the furniture!

Which Are Farm Animals?

Directions: Look at the pictures and name each animal. Then, decide which ones live on a farm. Do lambs live on a farm? "Yes." Do whales live on a farm? "No, they need to swim in the ocean!" Color the animals that could live on a farm. Put an **X** on the animals that do not usually live on a farm.

Look Around: Read a book about farm animals and talk about different animals you know and where they live.

Try This: Play a game where you call out a farm animal's name and you and your child make the sound of that animal and move like that animal moves.

Which Animals Can Fly?

Directions: Look at the pictures and name each animal. Then, decide which ones can fly. Can birds fly? Can frogs fly? Can dogs fly? Discuss what birds have to help them fly—wings! Put an **X** on the animals that cannot fly. Color the birds.

Look Around: Go outside and look for animals that can fly. What did you see?

Try This: Move your arms up and down and pretend to fly yourself. Can you flap your arms fast... then slow? Can you hold your arms out and glide like a hawk or an owl?

Which Animals Can Swim?

Directions: Look at the pictures and name each animal. Then, decide which ones can swim. Can fish swim? Can lizards swim? Discuss what animals have to help them swim—flippers and fins! Put an **X** on the animals that can't swim. Color the animals that swim.

Look Around: Go to an aquarium or fish store and watch animals swim.

Try This: Go to the library and find books about ocean animals.

Which Animals Can Run?

Directions: Look at the pictures and name each animal. Then, decide which ones can run. Can dogs run? "Yes." Can snakes run? "No, they have no legs—they slither." Can frogs run? Discuss what animals have to help them run—legs! Put an **X** on the animals that can't run. Color the animals that can run.

Look Around: Go outside and look for animals that can run. Find more animals that run in the stories you read.

Try This: Pretend to be dogs, cats, horses, or tigers. Make the sounds of each animal and then run like that animal would run.

Which Animals Are Small?

Directions: Name each animal. Some animals, like elephants, grow to be very large. Other animals are small. Look at the animals and decide which are large animals and which ones are smaller animals. Color the animals that are large.

Look Around: Compare the dogs you see when you go for a walk in your neighborhood. Which ones are small and which ones are large?

Try This: Ask your child to find something in his or her room that is small and something that is large.

110   ©*Teacher Created Resources*

Animals Have Families

Directions: Look at the farm animals below. Talk about the names of the baby animals and the adult animals. Trace the line to match each baby animal to its parent.

Look Around: Find some books to read about farm animal families and cuddle up and have a special reading time. Take turns making the sounds each farm animal makes.

Try This: Visit a farm or animal fair and observe animal families. Try to go in the spring.

Plants Are Living Things

Directions: Most plants need sunlight, water, and soil to stay healthy. Plants are living things. Some give us food. Farmers send the fruits and vegetables to the stores to sell. Color the fruit, the vegetables, and the flowers.

Look Around: Read a book about plants and growing things. Plant some seeds and see what you can grow!

Try This: Go on a plant hunt. If you can, find a fruit or a vegetable and pick it for a snack or dinner. If not, perhaps you can find flowers for the table.

Trees Are Living Things

Directions: Trees are big plants. They provide homes for many different animals. Find the animals living in the tree below and color them.

Look Around: See if you can see animals like squirrels or birds in trees in your yard.

Try This: Notice trees in your area. Talk about things that these trees provide such as beauty, food, scent, shade, privacy, wood, or homes for animals.

My Body Works

Directions: Look at the picture and name the child's different body parts. Talk about what each one does. "Hands help you pick things up. Feet and knees help you walk…." Color the picture.

Look Around: Stand together in front of a mirror. Try moving different body parts. Raise your arms. Clap your hands. Move your neck from side to side. Bend at the waist. Raise your legs.

Try This: Name a body part that helps you move and ask your child to point to it. Ask him or her to show you how it moves. Later, try to walk without bending your knees or wave without moving your shoulder or wrist.

Play and Rest

Directions: Together, look at the pictures and talk about what the children are doing. Talk about the active things you do each day and also about the restful things you do. Color the pictures.

Look Around: Go to the park and play. Talk about the different things you like to do to get exercise and how it makes you feel.

Try This: After a busy day, cuddle up and rest and read a special book. Talk about the activities of the day and how it is important to sleep so that you can have fun again tomorrow.

Five Senses

Directions: Our five senses help us learn. Talk about the picture below and how our senses help us discover more about our world. Read each word and help your child find the body part that helps with that sense.

See

Hear

Smell

Taste

Touch

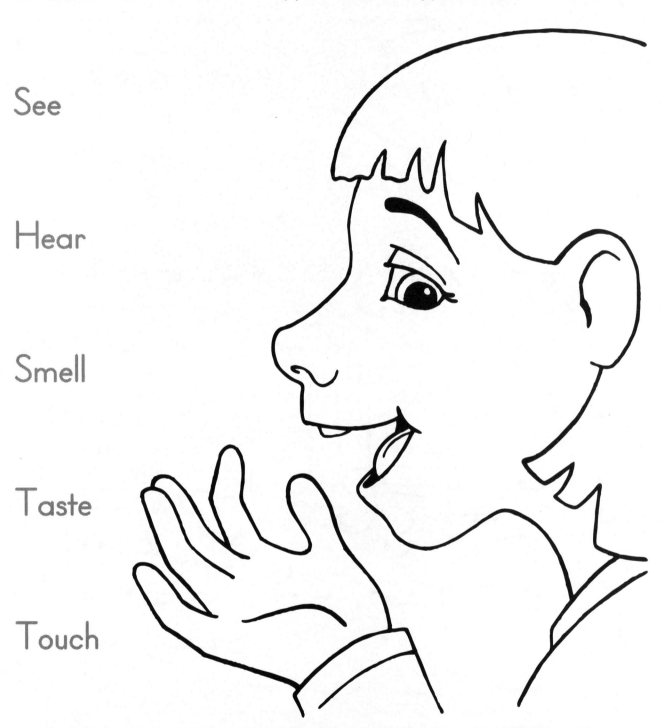

Look Around: Go outside and stand in one place. Use your senses to describe what you see, hear, feel, and smell. Is there something safe you can taste like an apple from a tree?

Try This: At dinner tonight, see how many of your five senses you and your child can use. How does dinner smell, taste, feel, and look? What can you hear? Is something crunchy or bubbly?

Fruits

Directions: Fruits are healthy foods. Together, name each fruit. Ask your child to color them and circle his or her favorite.

Look Around: Spend some time in the fruit section when grocery shopping together. Marvel at all the colors and shapes you see. How many can your child name?

Try This: The next time you are at a Farmers' Market together, taste test some fruits and pick out a new one to try!

Vegetables

Directions: Vegetables are healthy foods. Together, name each vegetable. Ask your child to color them and circle his or her favorite.

Look Around: Spend some time looking at vegetables when grocery shopping together. Marvel at all the colors and shapes you see. How many vegetables can your child name?

Try This: Make a salad together. See how many different vegetables you can add!

When It Is Hot

Directions: Notice the weather each day. On warm days, the sun shines brightly. Talk about the clothes you wear when it is sunny and what you like to do. Talk about what the children in the pictures are doing. Color the sun yellow.

Look Around: Read a book about the seasons or summertime play. What do you like to do when the sun is shining?

Try This: Water a plant or garden on a very sunny day. Talk about how plants and people need extra water to stay healthy when it is hot outside.

When It Snows

Directions: Talk to your child about snow. Explain that it is cold when it snows and you need to dress warmly to play in it. Talk about what the children are doing in the winter scene below. Ask your child to circle the activities he or she would like to do.

Look Around: What is the weather like today? Is there snow? If not, cuddle up and read books about snowy days. Talk about what you like or would like to do in the snow.

Try This: Together, enjoy or make popsicles, snow cones, or shave ices. Talk about how cold they are…. just like snow. Burrrrr.

When It Rains

Directions: What happens when rain falls from the clouds? Everything gets wet, the plants get watered, and puddles form! Look at the pictures below and color the things you wear when it rains.

Look Around: Look outside on a rainy day and watch the raindrops fall. Can you see raindrops dripping off the trees? Are there puddles forming?

Try This: Sing the rhyme, "Rain, Rain, Go Away." After it rains, go on a worm hunt! Look on sidewalks to see if any worms came up out of the wet ground!

Directions: Talk about your child and your family. How many people are in the family? What are their names? How old is each member? Help your child draw a stick figure for each person in your family. Use different shapes. Then circle the number of people in your family.

1 2 3 4 5 6

Look Around: Take some time to look at family pictures together. Talk about the different people in the pictures. Who is the oldest, biggest, youngest, etc.? Who lives in your house? Who visits?

Try This: Go to the library and find books about different families. Talk about the things in each story that are similar to your family and the things that are different.

What Is a Home?

Directions: Talk about your home and why it is special to you. Mention that it keeps you warm and dry, and then look at the pictures. Decide which house is a house for a bird, a dog, and a family. Draw a line from the house to who might live in it.

Look Around: Go for a walk and compare different homes to your home. What is the same about them and what is different?

Try This: Play in a tent or build a fort with your child. Decide what you want to have in your special house and set it up. Read a special book and sing some songs together.

The Rooms in a Home

Directions: Together, look at the pictures of things you find in a home. Name each item and talk about which room or rooms in a house it might go in. Color the items.

Look Around: Take a tour of your home together. Name each room and talk about what your family does there.

Try This: Ask your child to pick his or her favorite room and do something special in it—have a picnic, read a book about homes (animal or people), enjoy a nap, take a bath, or prepare a snack.

Family Jobs

Directions: Talk about taking care of the house. Use the pictures below to talk about different tasks that need to be taken care of. Ask your child to draw a line between the task on the left and the finished task on the right.

Look Around: Find a task in the house that your child can help you complete, and do it together.

Try This: Outside, are there leaves to be raked, flowers to be watered, or toys to be put away? Encourage your child to help you take care of his or her home by helping you.

Ways to Travel

Directions: Talk about the different ways we travel when it is too far to walk. Look at the pictures below and ask your child to color the pictures of vehicles he or she has ridden in or on.

Look Around: How do you and your child get from place to place each day? Does your vehicle have wheels? Do you ride with other people or just your family?

Try This: The next time you are out walking or in a vehicle, look for other means of transportation. Look for buses, trains, airplanes, and other options. Compare them.

Community Helpers

Directions: Let's look at the pictures and see if we know what job each person has. Then we can draw a line to the kind of vehicle each worker drives.

Look Around: Point out community helpers and their vehicles when you see them and talk about the jobs and the equipment used. Read a book about community helpers.

Try This: Try to visit a firehouse if there is one nearby. Look at the different kinds of trucks and equipment there. Find out what firefighters wear.

Work Vehicles

Directions: Look at the different vehicles below. Talk about what each vehicle is used for. Circle the vehicle you would like to work with when you grow up. Color the one you think would be the most fun.

Look Around: Go for a walk and see if you can find some work vehicles. What are they for and who uses them?

Try This: Pretend to be a worker for each vehicle above. Act out how each worker might use his or her vehicle at work.